AMERICA
MY DESTINY

BHARAT SHAH

ISBN: 149291889X
ISBN 13: 9781492918899

To my wife, Milan.

At our engagement, my father welcomed her into our family as Laxmi, goddess of wealth, happiness, and prosperity. She has proven herself to be all that and more!

Contents

Foreword

The book you are about to read is about a man and his family, his faith, his work, and his example. The story of Bharat Shah mimics, in some ways, the stories of many others who took advantage of the opportunities presented to them as they arrived on the shores of this great American country. However, there is something special about his story, and having the privilege of witnessing it gave me the honor of noting it here for all to read.

What is it that is so special about the competence, the love, the compassion, the success, the attention to parents, and the concern for peoplehood? What is it that is so special about courage, decency, and respect? What is so special is that it reminds us of what makes one human being's life worth getting to know. Bharat Shah's story is in fact a life exemplary, one that all should wish to imitate, not just for us but for those he most cares about. He has willed it with humility, not with ego.

As we observe all people, large and small, we only wish that Bharat's legacy would be theirs as well. His unselfish acts of leadership prove how one human being can succeed not by wounding others but by helping them.

My wish for the Shah's family is that his legacy would continue from generation to generation, that this story be told as the stories of the Upanishads are told so that the goodness and courage of this man would be remembered for all time.

Michael A. Leven
Friend

Mike Leven is a visionary who encouraged and guided Indian hoteliers for the formation of the Asian American Hotel Owners Association. Currently, he is president and chief operating officer of Sands Corporation, Las Vegas, Nevada.

A Word to the Reader

A few years back, at the age of twenty-four, my son Raj visited India for the first time. We were in my hometown of Navapur, visiting my parents' house where I grew up. Raj sat in dismay, looking at a narrow, three-room house, dark and dingy, with a bath area open to the sky. He turned to me and asked if I had really lived in the house for twenty-four years before leaving for America for higher studies. The answer was a proud yes! Then he remarked that now I live in a custom-built house surrounded by a golf course, lakes, and willow trees. The answer again was a proud yes! Shaking his head, he said he just could not believe it. Truthfully, the thought of making a comparison never hit me for as many times as I had visited my parents in the last few years. Both lifestyles had their own charm, except that I always felt lonely as I missed my parents and family when I returned to America.

Honestly, I did not leave India for higher education. I actually ran away from rampant corruption and discrimination in all its colors, which hindered personal growth. There was no place for a poor man's son to make anything of his life. Having passed through many phases of life, I have accepted discrimination as a universal phenomenon; and to some extent, this country is no exception. Still, it's only this place, the good old United States of America, where a risk taken at an opportune time and managed with hard work and honesty results in a dream fulfilled. One's color, creed, or anything else is not important.

Pursue a higher education—yes, I did. But that, in and of itself, did not result in financial independence. With regard to dreams, I did not have any. I just wanted to settle down with enough means to take care of my family. As new immigrants and a newly married couple, my wife, Milan, and I started our life together in an attic apartment. Milan stayed with me through thick and thin, during my life in the corporate world of the food industry as well as my failed attempts to become an importer of Indian goods. It was she who supported me in getting into the hospitality business as we put every penny we had at stake and stayed awake at night, worrying about making mortgage payments. As our business grew and money flow improved, we used it wisely and enjoyed life together with our sons, Mit and Raj.

It was Milan who encouraged our son Mit to join the family business. And it was Milan who held father's and son's hands for a smooth transfer of the business to the second generation. Mit has turned his father's humble beginnings into a nationally renowned institutional hospitality organization. Noble Investment Group is recognized for the depth of its strong team, its leadership in philanthropy and its strong investment returns through multiple decades and economic cycles.

Nowadays, when we recount those moments of twists and turns of life, when sometimes I laugh like crazy or tears roll from my eyes, Milan pleads with me to put it all on paper. Someday it may instill in someone a ray of hope that everything is possible in life. Just keep the faith.

This journey has been a wonderful experience for me, with plenty of personal challenges, financial as well as health related; having victories through perseverance; with enjoyment of family life with children and grandchildren; and fulfilling my earnest desire to be of service to my fellow human beings in whatever small ways that I could. It has been a very gratifying life indeed! We count so many blessings that have been bestowed upon us that at the end, it seems there is nothing left to complain about. My daily prayers reflect my ever-present gratitude.

CHAPTER 1
As the Wheel of Fortune Turned

Gujarat and Maharashtra are two neighboring states near the west coast of India. Navapur is a small town in Maharashtra, and Kadod is a small town in Gujarat; there is a distance of approximately forty miles between them. Navapur has a population of about twenty thousand, and the river Rangavali, a tributary of the major river Tapi, almost encircles the town. One of the major forests of India, the Dang jungle, is about fifty miles from Navapur. Lumber-related industries flourish, and cotton, lentils, and beans are major crops. Kadod is located on the banks of the Tapi, with a population of about twelve thousand. The town also has lumber-related businesses, with a major supply of timber coming from Navapur.

My grandfather Chunilal and grandma Jiji had settled in Navapur during the early 1900s. Grandfather was a visionary man of his time. He had focused on farming cotton on a large scale and investing in the cotton-related industry, ginning and pressing. He expanded his holdings by buying vast tracts of land and developing orchards around Navapur. He and my grandmother had ten children, five guys and five girls. The youngest among them, my father, was named Manu. When my father was eleven, my grandmother passed away as a result of a serious illness. My Aunt Suraj took my father to Bombay to take care of him; he grew up in Bombay and went to school there. My mother, Indu, was born and raised in Kadod. My maternal grandparents were Amrutlal and Jayaba. When my father was in his second year of college, he and my mother were married.

In the summer of 1935, my grandfather's business ran into trouble. His older sons, who were running the family business, had bought margins on cotton futures. When cotton prices tumbled, a call for money came to make up the shortfall. All the gold, orchards, and tracts of land that stretched for miles had to be sold to cover the shortfall. The family of Chunilal Shah declared bankruptcy. After all the transactions were complete, my parents were called to come to Navapur. The brothers had assembled to divide whatever was left behind. My parents received some broken utensils and old clothes as their share. My father felt betrayed by his older brothers. The story goes that he threw all the utensils on a street and burned the pile of old clothes in front of everybody. So it was that Chunilal's youngest son, once an heir to a multimillion-rupee fortune, and his newlywed wife were left homeless and penniless.

Dr. Bhangrej of Kadod, a close friend of my Grandpa Amrutlal, was building a temple in Navapur. He had built a small house next to the construction site to stay in whenever he visited the town to review the progress on the temple. My mother was like a daughter to him, as much as to her real father. Upon his arrival in town, Dr. Bhangrej called my parents to come and discuss the status of their life going forward. At the time, they were living with their jeweler friend, Ghelabhai. They had no other plans, except my father was waiting to hear from Navapur High School, where he had applied for a teaching position. Dr. Bhangrej gave them the keys to the house and asked them to move in right away. He also provided funds for them to buy utensils and groceries to settle down in the house.

The temple Dr. Bhangrej was building was for a Hindu deity, Lord Dattatraya, a Trinity. It is a philosophical manifestation of Brahma, the creator of life; Vishnu, the preserver of life; and Shiva, the protector of the soul as it passes from one birth to the next through the process of reincarnation. It is the essence of Hindu religion and philosophy. My parents considered the gift from Dr. Bhangrej a lifetime event and a great blessing from Lord Dattatraya, and thus both of them became devout followers of the Trinity. That is the house where my brother, my sisters, and I were born and grew up. Saryu, my older sister, was born in 1937; I arrived in 1939; and a year later, my sister Kunju was born. Malini, our baby sister, was born twelve years later and our brother Sanjay fifteen years later. All of us children called our parents Pappa and Ba.

Navapur Home

My father finally received a teacher's assignment at Navapur High School. He taught English and math, his two favorite subjects. Our family was getting settled, to a certain extent. As the youngest child of a wealthy man, my father's life in the big city of Bombay had been full of social activities. He had developed hobbies, such as playing bridge and participating in plays, taking on lead roles. A few blocks from our home was a bridge club where the businessmen of Navapur and government officers spent their evenings. On one chance occasion, my father met a forest ranger who was in charge of Dang Jungle operations, and an opportunity to become a lumber businessman opened. Hardly a year after starting work as a teacher, my father resigned from the school and became a full-fledged businessman.

As the business flourished and money flowed in, managing the family expenses was not difficult. Mother's wardrobe got updated with new saris and jewelry. The money cabinet was filled to the brim; there was no bank in town to deposit cash. Our new prosperity was very visible. Navapur had about four or five cars in all, and we had one of them, a 1942 Ford convertible. Our chauffer, Shivram, was driving Pappa around, especially for long trips. Our in-house chef, Bhikhu, the best cook in town, was making two meals a day. At that time my sister Saryu was about twelve years old, I was ten, and Kunju was nine. We kids were having the time of our lives.

The lumber business expanded year after year. The largest and potentially the most profitable venture of Pappa's life was a lease contract to cut trees from 100,000 acres of teakwood forest known as the Sagbara Jungle, owned by the king of Sagbara Estate. Pappa signed the contract in 1958 and established an operational infrastructure, pending approval from the government of Gujarat, to cut the trees.

Pappa encouraged my mother to run for town council. He tutored her on how to tackle various issues, give statements, and be a real politician. Mother turned out to be a powerful speaker. When she was delivering her speech onstage, we kids would look at her in awe, thinking, *That's our mother!* She got elected as a town councilwoman for a five-year term.

Besides giving good speeches, my mother had other talents. She was a good cook, always interested in trying new recipes, and she was probably the fastest knitter I've ever known. She would have a bundle of woolen threads of different colors to make a sweater, and after seeing a person in the morning, she would have a beautiful sweater whipped out by the evening, all hand-knitted.

My father was a very well-educated man for his time. He was a college student at University of Bombay when he had to return to Navapur to settle family's financial troubles. He subscribed to many newspapers and business magazines. Once he attended a Rotary Club meeting in Bombay and, understanding its reputation in the business world, he founded the Rotary Club of Navapur. The town's business sector revived with a buzz of new activities. Pappa was an influential man in many local and state elections. People followed his directives in planning and executing their campaign strategies.

Pappa was also a founding member of the Navapur Drama Club. In one of the plays he was a *diwan*, a secretary of state, a home minister of a kingdom. A multifaceted, multitalented *diwan* had turned the kingdom from a tyrant state to a very happy place to live in for the common man. The play received many state and national awards. Pappa's last name thereafter was changed to Diwan; he was known as Manubhai Diwan.

Another of my father's hobbies was astrology. Given a person's place, date, and time of birth, he could draw a birth chart using the Indian astrological tables. His predictions were mostly correct, based on various aspects of planetary positions. Visitors flocked to my home from all parts of the country. The generous aspect of his hobby was that he never charged a penny for his readings. If anyone insisted on donating money for his services, he would recommend that the person send it to the charity of his or her choice. My father loved to help anyone who desired educational progress in choosing a career or in gaining college admission with scholarship funds. He had a collection of books that listed colleges all around India, along with their admission policies and the formalities involved in applying for scholarships. Students and their parents would come to him to get advice. Once a student was ready to leave town for further studies, my house would be the first place he or she would stop to pay respects. My father felt very gratified by the love he received from the community he had helped.

Around the middle of 1950, my parents learned of a Swami, a holy man, known as Shri Rang Avdhut. He was a follower of Lord Dattatraya, the Trinity. He had an ashram at Nareshvar on the banks of the river Narmada. One day my parents and a few friends traveled to Nareshvar, arriving there at night. The next morning the group had a *darshan*, a meeting, with Rang Avdhut. The group was awed by his simplicity, devotion to God in all its forms, and philosophy of nondiscrimination toward all religions of the world. His message was that God resides within oneself. The theme of his message was "Paraspar Devo Bhava"—to look for godliness within each of us. There was no self-promotion. Rang Avdhut would not accept any money or rice as an offering. If someone wanted to donate anything, he or she could do so at the common kitchen. One could donate money, grains, groceries, utensils, or just labor to help prepare food for the visitors.

Rang Avdhut was lovingly called Bapji, a fatherly figure who would give proper guidance. He was a learned man with a penchant for poetry. At the request of one of his followers, he had written a poem called "Dattabavni." The poem has fifty-two lines in praise of Lord Dattatraya and various other incarnations of Hindu gods, such as Ram and Krishna. It is a widely held belief that the Dattabavni is a powerful prayer that brings peace and happiness to one who recites it. My parents became devout followers of Rang Avdhut, and all of us children also followed the path growing up.

CHAPTER 2
Childhood Memories

When our sons, Mit and Raj, were growing up, occasionally they got into some mischief. My wife, Milan, would complain, and my answer always was that she had not heard about the mischief I got into during my childhood. She needed to hear that from my mother! Our boys were far better than their dad. Now I am a grandfather. Mit has a sixteen-year-old son, Arjun. Mit's wife, Reshma, would complain to me from time to time of Arjun being rambunctious and ask me what to do. I always wanted to tell her to get a rope like Arjun's great-grandmother did. Instead, I would calm her down and say, "Reshma, it runs in the genes! Only time will take care of it."

My mischief making knew no bounds, and a rope around a pipe in my house in Navapur was a standard fixture. When Saryu, Kunju, and I would arrive home from school, Saryu would fix a snack for us. Invariably, I would complain of something not being right. If the girls gave me any backtalk, I threw the whole plate against a wall in the kitchen. Mother would hear the commotion and come into the kitchen and see the broken pieces of glass everywhere. She would drag me to the pipe and tie the rope around my wrists. Mother would wait for my father to arrive home, and then all hell would break loose. I would get beaten up bad!

Mischievous acts also led to lies. One time I was sick and was supposed to take a regular dose of liquid medicine. One night before going to bed, my parents saw that I was not taking the medication properly and that the bottle was quite full. When I woke up in the morning, it dawned on me that the bottle looked quite full, so I drained some liquid to be correct on the doses. That morning, my father reminded me very casually that I should take the medications on time. I said I do. He looked at the bottle and knew I had tampered with it. After repeated questioning and my staying firm that I was telling truth, he asked me to take an oath by putting my hand on a photo of the Trinity. In Hinduism, the belief is that if one is not telling the truth and takes an oath on someone very important in the family, for example the person's son, the son will die. Thinking quickly that God never dies, I laid my hand on the photo. Not so smart as I was immediately kicked out of the house! My sisters were asked to disown me as their brother. Because I teased Kunju so much, she was fine with me being gone from the house. Saryu asked me whether I was lying, and I embarrassedly told her yes. She pleaded with Pappa, and, because of that, I was allowed to reenter the house.

When I was around the age of twelve, a few of us guys were playing on a street. A couple of horses were standing in a corner, their reins in the hands of a caretaker. We went behind the horses and started whacking them slightly from the back. One horse kicked back toward us but did not touch anybody. I decided to hit it hard, and the horse kicked back so quickly that I got hit on my forehead. I went down and started bleeding heavy. My father's bridge club was close by, and someone ran and brought him to the site. By the time he arrived, I was unconscious. In those days Navapur had no doctors; the only thing we had was a government clinic at the end of the town. My father carried me in his arms to the clinic. Dr. Joglekar was the attending physician. He put a bandage on the wound and gave me some medications. Penicillin had just been invented, but Navapur did not have any pharmacies. The city of Surat, a four-hour train ride from Navapur, was the closest source. Navapur had no electricity and hence no refrigerators. The vials of penicillin were packed in ice and brought to us in thermos bottles every day. I was unconscious for about three days; my mother told me that they had no hope of my survival. Dr. Joglekar was a godsend. He visited us three times a day and made sure I was not running a fever, a sign of infection. I recovered fully after a couple of months in bed. The scar above my forehead is still visible. I believe that after this major incident, I probably calmed down, and my mischief making decreased.

Now I needed other outlets for my energy. Bhuso was a houseman from my grandfather's time. He just loved me. He was the one who could save me from my father's rage if my mischief had crossed my mother's line. There was a Shiva temple on the banks of the river Rangavali; a five minute walk from my house. Every Saturday morning, in front of the temple, there would be free wrestling matches. When I was about ten, Bhuso began to take me to the temple. Guys of all ages would get together to compete, and Bhuso would instruct me on whom to challenge. Judges would make sure that guys of equal age competed in the match. The winner received a coconut as a trophy. I wrestled there many times and brought home lots of coconuts.

I was the only boy in the family at that time but was lucky enough to have an older male sibling figure to guide and mentor me. My father had a sister, Dhiraj, who lived in town. Among all the siblings, Pappa and Dhiraj had the best relationship. Dhiraj's eldest son, Rajni, was a favorite of my father. Rajni was like his own son and about fifteen years my senior. I grew up considering him my older brother and calling him Rajnibhai. He was the life of the party and a driving force behind all cultural and sporting activities in Navapur. Rajnibhai took me under his wing; I attended all his parties and learned DJ-ing skills at a very young age. He was a founder of the Navbharat Cricket Club and a captain of the "A" team. I played on the "C" team but was invited to play on his team as a junior player.

I had an interest in acting and had developed drama skills from a very young age—not surprising, as it ran in the family. There was a play called *Rupaiya*, a one-rupee coin. My class teacher selected me to play the main character, a boy whose sister wanted to celebrate his birthday. This was my first attempt at drama. Prabha, a girl in my class, was selected as my sister, and a few classmates were chosen to be my friends. In the story, my sister convinces my friends to contribute one rupee each to celebrate my birthday, which becomes a very joyous event. On opening night, we stormed the stage; all the participants played their parts well. Prabha and I proved to be natural actors. The play was very well received. We repeated the play at a moment's notice whenever the school principal had a visitor who needed to be impressed by the school's cultural activities.

Every summer, my sister Saryu and I would travel down to Kadod to visit our grandparents. As an unspoken tradition, we would enter from the backyard with our backpacks. Grandma Jayaba loved us being there for vacations; and Grandpa Amrutdada, a great soul, looked forward to my coming to Kadod. He would wait for my arrival before planning a trip to the farms, about four to five hours' ride in a bullock cart, for harvesting mangos and other fruit crops. A couple of days after my arrival, the two of us would leave for the farms.

In the early years, I would play with Saryu and her friends. As I grew older, I started making my own friends on the street. The river Tapi was about ten minutes' walk from our neighborhood, and a favorite pastime was to roll up a towel with a change of clothes and head down to Tapi for a morning swim. After a good lunch, I would be on the street, playing and competing with other guys with marbles, spinning tops and seashells. My winnings were so large that Grandma Jayaba had to use large jars and tin boxes to store all my treasures.

On my grandparents' street in Kadod, there was a family that had a wholesale lumber shop. The head of this family was Kantibhai. He had come to know that Amrutlal's son-in-law was in the lumber business in Navapur. During one of our family visits to Kadod, Kantibhai invited my parents to tea at his house. My father and Kantibhai quickly took a liking to each other. Both were the same age, enjoyed tasty food, and were great card players. As time went on, the two families became very close. Kantibhai had no sisters, and as my mother, Indu, was from Kadod, they shared a strong kinship. Kantibhai had asked my mother to be his sister in life. That made him Kantimama (maternal Uncle) and his wife Ushamami (maternal aunt) for Saryu, Kunju and I. Their children became our cousins.

I played three-card poker with seashells for chips. One day I was at a poker game, and just as the cards were dealt, I was about to pick up my three cards to see what I had. An elderly voice came from above my shoulder and advised me to play blind. Blind play keeps you in the game at half the cost while anyone who wants to continue playing has to double the bet. My teacher advising from behind was none other than Kantimama. He was very proud of me. He had recognized that even at such a young age, and in addition to being an out-of-towner, I had gained quite a respected reputation on the streets of Kadod.

Returning to Navapur after our vacations in Kadod was always very tough. My father was a disciplinarian. Everything had to be done on time; our grades had to be at the top of the class; and if our teachers did not give us enough homework, there would be more at home. Pappa, the in-house math professor, had a strict routine for us. Usually, after supper at night, Saryu, Kunju, and I would sit in a row. We recited the multiplication tables from two through twenty. Saryu and Kunju were allowed to leave at that point, but I had to continue with twenty-one, thirty-one, and the tables for fractions. No mistakes were allowed.

Each Saturday we had school in the morning. Friday afternoon Saryu and I would get a topic from each of our classes for a debate the next morning. On Friday nights Pappa would ask us for the topics and ask us individually whether we were "for" or "against" the issue. Participation in a class debate was mandatory at my home. Saryu would state her position on her class topic, and I would state mine. Then Pappa would spend time with each of us, discussing the topic and why we were in favor or against the issue. Thereafter, he would give his opposing views on the topics and prepare us for a rebuttal at the end of the debates. Saryu and I became well known for our accomplished vocabulary as a result of grueling exercises.

When I was about thirteen, Saryu was engaged to Chandrakant, a young man from a well-to-do family in Navapur. Chandrakant gave me banjo as a gift. One day I was playing the banjo on my front porch, and a boy name Raghu who lived nearby asked me if he could play. Raghu turned out to be an accomplished banjo player. He had a style of striking the strings that created very smooth music, so I asked him to teach me one song. He found an easy one for me to practice and showed me how to transition smoothly from one key to another. I picked up on his style, and my music, like his, was soon very pleasing. My hobby of banjo playing continued, including public performances, through high school and college. My skills in drama, music, debates, and leadership resulted in my being recognized, especially by girls, at an early age.

Among my early friends was my cousin Lalit, who was from Bombay. He had moved to Navapur to live with his uncle and to go to school there.

Pravin, nicknamed Kinu, was my classmate and a good friend. Dilip, Dipak, and Harish, three cousins who lived together in a joint family, and their friends Vinod, Naresh, and Navin were a group of six. When I joined them, it made a "Gang of Seven." At about age thirteen, I went to Bombay with Lalit for a short vacation. His family lived in a multifamily apartment building. Lalit's brother and other children in the building played games together, such as hide-and-seek. I noticed that there was one girl who liked to hang around me. One day, while the two of us were in a corner by ourselves, she kissed me right on the lips! That was the first time in my life that I was kissed by a girl. That made the vacation in Bombay that much more special and memorable. A country boy from Navapur learned a few things from a city girl. When I returned to Navapur, I bragged about my experience to the Gang of Seven.

Now at school in Navapur, I was looking at girls from a different perspective. I tried to get close to the girls in my class and sought their friendship. I had developed a reputation of being a top-notch student and a good leader. Some of the guys and girls in the class had started asking me for advice on school homework and solving math problems. Recognizing my popularity in the class, I developed an interest in becoming a class monitor. The position had an authority over the class in the absence of a teacher. That year, in grade nine, I decided to run for class monitor. We were thirty-five students in the class, about twelve girls and twenty-three boys. There were three of us competing. I was elected as a result of the entire block of girls voting in my favor. I continued to be the class monitor for four years, until I graduated from high school. During the teacher's absence, it was the monitor's job to keep discipline in the class. Those who made noise, talked, or created any disturbance had their names written on the back of the blackboard and turned over to the teacher for appropriate punishment. The girls were always excused for obvious reasons: it was political payoff time!

My friendship with the girls in the class grew closer. One day two of the girls, Rama and Shaku, brought some snacks to school and invited my friend Kinu and me to share with them during our afternoon recess. We walked outside the school campus and found a corner to sit and share the goodies. Each afternoon thereafter, we followed the same schedule.

Kinu and I would start walking first, and after a few steps, our snack partners would follow us. At the end of recess, we all would slowly drift back toward the class. One day Saryu and her friends observed my "special break" with the girls. When Saryu got home, she complained to our parents. Mother was furious; Pappa just walked away smiling. To my dismay, however, and to Saryu's pleasure, the snack breaks ended!

To my father, playing poker, using timely cursing, learning how to drive on your own without a license, having girlfriends to feed you snacks, being a leader in all undertakings, and all related attributes were boy things to do. Lacking in leadership qualities or having an indecisive mind was absolutely not allowed. Period.

Bharat at Sixteen

The last two years of high school were important, and Pappa kept close track of my grades. If I needed any help with a subject, he was always there. During those years, studies took precedence over all my other activities. In March 1956, all the class students went to Surat for the state-level high school diploma examination. Rama, Shaku, Kinu, and I traveled together and kept in touch with each other during the week-long examinations. All of us did well and returned to Navapur. Kinu and I had done very well in all subjects. Both of us received excellent grades and were accepted at Wilson College, University of Bombay. Pretty soon, the country boys left for the big city of Bombay. Following the conservative traditions of their families, Rama and Shaku remained in Navapur and did not pursue a college education.

Over the next summers my two snack partners got married. Rama, at age seventeen and Shaku a year later at age eighteen. I lost contact with them for a number of years. I visited both Shaku and Rama during my recent trip to India, almost fifty-five years after being high school class-mates. Shaku is a widow, living in Baroda with her daughter. Rama lives in a suburb of Bombay with her husband, Jitubhai. I could feel that although our lives have taken us in different directions and in different parts of the world, the glue that binds us together was still there. I could feel the same innocent kindness and affection I felt as a teenager. It was good to see that all of us had aged gracefully and the fond memories of the "good old days" still lingered with us.

CHAPTER 3
Bombay, Here I Come!

During June of 1956, Satish, Kinu, and I, three of the top students of Navapur High, arrived in Bombay to attend Wilson College. All three of us became roommates at Mackichan Hall, the dormitory just across from the entrance to the college.

Our very first class was English Literature. As the first-bench students of Navapur High, we sat in the front of the class. We had a reputation to maintain! The teacher, a Scottish lady, entered the classroom and immediately began reading from a textbook in a heavy accent. It was a two-hundred-page book, and for the entire forty-five minutes, we all kept flipping through pages to find out which page she was on. No luck. At the end of the class, we tried to chase her down, like beggars after food, to ask what chapter she had read so we could prepare for the next class. She had no time for us. With a stern look on her face, she said something we didn't understand and just walked away.

In Navapur, we had been taught English as a second language, starting in grade seven. So, basically, we arrived in Bombay with fifth-grade English and were trying to cope with college-level English in an indecipherable Scottish accent. We were doomed to fail! We returned to our room in silence, with heavy hearts. There was nobody to help us and give us advice; we felt abandoned. Kinu and I just burst out crying. What madness it had been to come to Bombay! There was no way we would even pass our freshman year. What a shock to the top of the class of Navapur High School. Gulab Shah, a year senior to us, was in the room next to ours. We had met him a couple of times. That evening he came to our room to check on us. We started sobbing again. He sat on the bed and calmed us down, telling us that other professors were from India, and we would not have any difficulty understanding them. As for the Scottish teacher, we would not have to deal with her after the first year. Besides, he said, he was there to help us if we had difficulty understanding any subject.

During the first month or so, Satish, Kinu, and I each found our own friends. I was hanging out with Gulab and his friends. Gulab loved movies and music. He was very good in chemistry and physics and became my tutor for those subjects. His friend Raman Patel was good in math. Raman was very good at giving advice with a calming effect, almost with spiritual overtones. We called him "Kaka" (Uncle), and I went to him for any difficulties I had, educational or otherwise. With my limited English vocabulary, it was difficult to understand the principles behind any chemistry or physics theory. I would read a chapter at least ten times, looking in a dictionary for words I did not know to make some sense of the main theme of the chapter. I would have to work at least 5-10 times harder and I was prepared to do that to maintain good grades. Satish and Kinu coped in their own ways.

Mackichan Hall had two cafeterias or mess halls as they called it: one vegetarian, the other nonvegetarian. All of us being Hindu, we had joined the vegetarian mess. I did not like the food much; I had been spoiled by my sisters. A friend I made through Gulab was Hussein Pothiawala. Hussein was a Muslim and was a member of the non-vegetarian cafe. One day I complained to him about the quality of food at the vegetarian mess, saying that it was very bland. Hussein invited me to join him as a guest one day at his mess. I insisted that he not let me eat any meat, knowingly or unknowingly. He promised. Thereafter, I visited his mess many times as a guest. One evening a server brought a plate that looked different. I asked what it was. Before the server could answer, Hussein said it was mung bean. I ate the "mung bean" like crazy; the spicy mix went very well with chapatti and rice. After dinner, Hussein asked me if I liked their "mung bean." I said it was great and that somehow the vegetarian mess did not make such good, spicy dishes. He told me I had actually had a non-vegetarian dish called *khima*, made with ground lamb. That was the day a purely vegetarian Hindu became non-vegetarian.

As a newcomer to Bombay, I carefully observed the dressing and grooming styles of the locals. I noticed that a college senior who lived at my dorm was always the best-dressed. Every day, going to classes, he wore new slacks, a well-pressed shirt, shiny shoes, and a belt. He was very reserved but elicited a sense of respect from other students and the dorm superintendent. One evening I asked him to help me with my clothes and accessories. He was very happy about the compliment and introduced me to his master tailor. In no time my wardrobe was upgraded, and I was transformed into a Bombay Boy.

I started getting noticed, getting compliments from the friends I had already made and a few new ones who wanted to be my friends. One group that noticed me was several girls who sat on the side porch at the entrance of the college. This group of about ten to twelve girls and their leader, Shoba Khote, would tease boys passing by with all kind of titles. Shoba was a senior at college and acted in Indian cinema in various lead and supporting roles. We had teased girls in Navapur, but I had never experienced the reverse role. One morning as I was walking toward this gang, with my head down, one girl remarked, "Hey, Dev Anand is coming." All the girls turned their heads, looked at me, and smiled. Then one girl said in a somewhat serious tone in the Marathi language, "He really does look like Dev Anand." I was a shy freshman and couldn't even look up. Dev Anand was one of my favorite Indian cinema actors, and this was the second time I had heard the compliment. When I was about fourteen, one of my sister Saryu's friends had remarked on my resemblance to Dev Anand. That had been good to hear, but I liked hearing it from one of the college girls much better.

As a part of the Diwali celebrations, Mackichan Hall had a musical evening. I had entered the program to play the banjo. When my turn came, I went onstage and played a fast, melodious tune. The audience was on their feet. I was asked to play one more song and repeated the same level of performance. From that day on, my reputation and recognition among other students at the dorm was on the rise. Wilson College was near a few professional cultural and art centers. I attended many performances, especially drama. I was very much impressed with the artists of Bombay. I learned a lot from their style of acting and delivery.

When I arrived home for Diwali vacation, my mother was happy to see me. Pappa was pleased, as my attire, hairstyle, and mannerisms had developed to a class that was to his liking. The main issue was my studies and he of course wanted to know how I was doing. I did not want to disappoint him, and I said fine, not wanting to scare him with my problems with English. I felt that, in time, I would do fine. The Navbharat club, under the leadership of Rajnibhai, had a regional drama competition in Navapur. The teams, judges, and audience came from towns both nearby and as far away as Surat. I was given a lead role in one drama. Navin, my friend from the Gang of Seven, was my sidekick. After three days of competition, I was awarded the top prize. An older boy who had led a university team for a national drama competition had been favored to win the Navapur drama competition. My new acquired skills from Bombay worked. At the young age of seventeen, I beat a university pro.

My home in Navapur was buzzing with activities. My father's business was in high gear; the lumberyard at the railroad station was the largest I had ever seen. The money cabinet was packed so full that when I opened the cabinet to get a few rupees, bundles of hundred-rupee bills would fall out. Mother looked happy. Pappa had lots of visitors each day. Some came for business transactions, some to get readings on astrological charts, and some for guidance on election strategy. Pappa was a kingmaker for local and state government elections. The family of Manubhai Diwan was at its zenith in Navapur. Deep in his heart, my father was a family man. The year 1957 had to be his most successful financial year. He decided to take a long family vacation; we would travel all the way to Kashmir. Plans were made to prepare the 1942 Ford convertible to make the trip. Shivram, the driver, and Bhikhu, the cook, were included in the party with my parents, Saryu, Kunju, young Malini, baby Sanjay, and me. That month of family vacation was the best ever. We visited Delhi, Agra, to see the Taj Mahal on our way to Srinagar, the capital of Kashmir. In Srinagar we stayed in a houseboat on the famous Dal Lake for two weeks. When we returned home, we all had rosy cheeks and looked great as a result of Kashmir's clean, beautiful atmosphere.

After we got home, it was time to return to college. This year my sister Kunju and my friend Dilip had both received their high school diplomas and were leaving for college. Kunju was to study in Surat, and Dilip was going to Baroda. Pappa asked me to accompany Kunju and to settle her down in a dorm before I could leave for Bombay for my sophomore year. On a train to Surat, I convinced Kunju that she would not need my help. The poor girl did not argue. I traveled with Dilip to Baroda and spent a couple of days to help him settle. We had fun watching movies and visiting various restaurants. On the way to Bombay, I did not even stop in Surat to check how Kunju was doing. Within a week I had a sixteen-page letter from my father. He was angry that I had shirked my responsibility to my younger sister. There was a message on family values and the need for an older brother's commitment to caring for all siblings. I never replied to the letter, but in my heart I made a lifetime promise to follow his directives. Whenever I have felt the need to help a family member, whether I was asked for help or not, my father's letter has always come to my mind, influencing my heart. As if he were still alive, I would tell him not to worry and that I would take care of it. It is the same message I have passed on to my sons, Mit and Raj, while the two of them were growing up—and even now that they are adults..

My sophomore year in college was very important. The final grades at the year's end would be the ticket for acceptance into medical or engineering school. A student wishing to become a doctor would take biological science as a major; a student going into the engineering field would select math as a major. Satish and I returned to Bombay and chose math as our majors. Kinu decided, very wisely, not to return to Bombay and instead went to Baroda to continue his college education. My goal was to become a mechanical engineer. Top grades were necessary to gain admission into engineering college. My level of English had not improved much. I would still read a chapter many times but be unable to master the subject. I could not keep a conversation going in English. I would give "yes" or "no" answers, or at the most I might be able to handle some short sentences without any grammar fundamentals. My struggle with my studies continued.

The sophomore class held a picnic that year. A few guys and girls got together and traveled by bus to a picnic spot. As the bus started, I took out my banjo, and a classmate opened a *dholak* (a drum), and the two of us soon had everybody on their feet, dancing. As we approached the destination, I began to put my banjo away; and a very pretty, tall, slim girl came up to me and said her name was Hema. Before I had a chance to reply, she jumped into my lap, hugged me hard, and gave me two or three quick kisses. I did not know what to do, so I remained still and silent. Having gotten no response from me, she left me alone for the rest of the day. Later on I found out that besides being a college student, she modeled for a famous sari house. Knowing what her profession was, this country boy convinced himself that this really was not a game for him. I felt that it could actually create larger problems in the future, mainly with my studies. One thing was for sure, my mother did not have to worry about my extracurricular activities. Except for watching girls on campus and on the beaches of Bombay, I made no serious attempt to get involved. Basically, there was no time for it. I was scared that if I did so, I might mess up my grades even worse, and Navapur might start looking down on me. However, for more reasons than one, that was not to be.

After a few months in Bombay, I returned to Navapur for a vacation. Dilip returned from Baroda. The Gang of Seven started working on a picnic plan. I suggested the menu include a chicken curry. The Hindu guys got scared, but I convinced them that we would be all right. We found a Muslim friend and gave him money to get chicken curry prepared at his home and to deliver it to us at night behind a particular building, from where the entourage would head to a riverbank for the special picnic. Somehow, news of the picnic menu was leaked in town. The next morning Dilip and I were walking around town, and everyone who saw us gave us a mean look, and some people made sarcastic comments. When we approached Rajnibhai's house, he was standing on the front porch, and he was furious. He said, "If this is what you learn in college, shame on you!" He somehow knew I had been the main architect of the picnic menu. From that day on, for many long years, Rajnibhai wrote me off: Bharat was not good company.

Family Vacation 1957

Later on in the evening, a few of the town's elders and Saryu's husband, Chandrakant, came to see my father. I was sitting on the front porch. I knew why they were there because, coming up the steps, no one greeted me or looked at me, and that was unusual. Instead of leaving home to meet up with the gang, I sat on the porch, scared of what was to happen next. I was worried I might get kicked out of the house again. When the group left, my father came and sat next to me and put a hand on my shoulder. Looking into my eyes, he said, "Why do you have to let the whole damn town know what you guys are doing at a picnic? Keep all that quiet next time." That was it! That was him. He was the man who believed in personal freedom and allowed his children to make their own choices. I also felt that being a college student, his relationship with me had changed to that of a friend rather than an authoritative father. Outside of our home, however, within the Hindu community, I had lost some respect. A Hindu eating chicken curry was a crime as serious as being a drug addict.

After vacation, I returned to Bombay to the same strenuous environment that I had left behind. I buckled down to my studies and waited for the final exams. The result was not any better than my freshman year; I barely passed and thus, failed to enter medical or engineering college. The reputation I carried in high school got wiped out in less than two years.

My junior year in college was not all that demanding. Cultural and social activities increased during that year. I was elected general secretary of Mackichan Hall. That meant that I was the chief operating officer of the dormitory. The activity center, operations of the messes, general upkeep, and maintenance were under my supervision. I revised the operations of the kitchen, took control of the money, and improved food quality without raising membership fees. I organized many entertainment events while I was in charge, including the annual musical program. I initiated a beautification program whereby all unused land around the dormitory received new landscaping and flower beds. Forty years later, in 1998, I visited Mackichan Hall with my son Raj. It was heartwarming that the landscaping project that I had initiated was still being maintained.

My senior year was devoted to my studies to get a degree certificate. I had improved my grades during the year and received a Bachelor of

Science degree in 1960. My major was chemistry, with physics as a minor. That accomplishment was nothing to brag about. A top student from Navapur High School was expected to become an engineer or a doctor. I did not attend the graduation ceremony and returned home with mixed emotions.

CHAPTER 4
Sailing in Uncharted Waters

During 1958, Pappa signed a contract to lumber 100,000 acres of forest, mostly teak, near the town of Sagbara in Gujarat. He went to Ahmedabad, capital of Gujarat, to apply for a permit to cut trees. This was a large project, and the Ministry of Interior was immediately informed. Pappa was called in to meet the Minister. Behind closed doors, the Minister asked for one million rupees to approve the permit process. Pappa countered by offering even more but in installments as the cutting progressed each year. The offer was rejected. Pappa did not have that much cash available from his business, and the Minister remained adamant. Years passed, but the impasse remained unresolved.

Little did I know that in 1958 while I was a sophomore at Wilson College, Pappa was laying a foundation for my future business plans. While studying various business magazines, he had come upon a patent available for commercial application to manufacture fruit juice powders. My father's business sense told him that with the large population of India, there would be a great market for any good-quality food product. The process was developed by the scientists at Central Food Technological Research Institute in Mysore, a city in southern India. Pappa acquired the rights to the patent. My career path and future business plans were sealed at that point. That year Pappa selected a site for the plant in Pardi, a small town near the city of Bulsar, in the state of Gujarat. The government of Gujarat had approved an 80 percent loan for a project costing one million rupees, and the plant construction began that year.

With a Bachelor of Science degree in hand, one day in August of 1960, I left by train to Mysore. The Central Food Technological Research

Institute (CFTRI) was a world-renowned institution. The main campus building was originally a summer palace of the Maharaja of Mysore. After completing the admissions paperwork, I found out that there were going to be sixteen students in my class. No one had arrived yet. In Mysore, people spoke the local language, Kanada, which I did not know. There are twenty-eight states in India and each one has its own regional language. I was a stranger in my own country. I found the food dishes unfamiliar and unpleasant to look at.

A diploma in food science and technology would be awarded after two years of learning methods of food preservation—canning, freezing, dehydration, and radiation technology. I would be trained in production of fruit juice powders as a part of a special study. The medium of instruction was English. As all students came from various states, each one spoke his own language. Therefore, our personal conversation was done either in Hindi or in English. Because of that, my conversational English improved.

In Mysore, my focus was on studying. Each day after the classes and lab, I would spend a lot of time in the library, reading various methods of food preservation, the latest research on processing methods, and upcoming technologies. A few months after the classes started, there was a short Diwali vacation for the students. I stayed at school to learn the process to manufacture fruit juice powders. Through my reading, I found out that the process was originally developed and patented in 1947 by scientists in the United States of America. In 1953, the patent was declared commercially nonviable by the US scientists. Indian scientists at CFTRI had made a few insignificant changes to the process and had received an Indian patent in 1956, and Pappa bought the patent rights in 1958. How would a lumber businessman know the intricacies of evaluating a technical process? He was just trying to help his son become an entrepreneur. After a year and a half of study, a tour of food manufacturing plants all over India, and three months of plant experience, I received a diploma in food science and technology.

At the end of two years, I was bringing home a better understanding of our project and a few new ideas for future development of the food industry in India. The market study that I had read showed that the consumption of poultry and eggs, and thus poultry farming, in India would rise to greater heights in a few years. Another consumer need with a greater demand that showed a bright future on the horizon was bottled water, as the ever-growing middle class would demand clean water. I brought complete files on the projects with me to Navapur. This was 1962. I was a young man of twenty-two with the enthusiasm to become an up-and-coming entrepreneur, something that Pappa had expected of me but never expressed.

That year the Diwali atmosphere in Navapur was, as always, very festive. My friends were happy to see me in town after two years of absence. We were back together again, making plans for picnics, parties, and playing cards. The atmosphere at my home, however, was subdued. There was a lot of tension in the air. The money cabinet was telling a story. Two years earlier, before leaving for Mysore, I had seen it overflowing with bundles of hundred-rupee bills. Now it was nearly empty, with only a few bundles left on one of the shelves.

Sagbara had become the main focus of activity. The impasse between the minister asking for one million rupees under the table and my father countering with payments of regular installments had not been resolved. Sometime in 1959 my father sued the government of Gujarat for withholding the permit to cut the trees. There were a plethora of barristers and attorneys that were hired to fight the case: barristers Nuri and Parikh in Bombay, Kazi in Surat, and Vakharia in Ahmedabad. I accompanied Pappa for many consultation meetings in Bombay at Nuri's residence. I was too young and naïve to understand the legal issues of the time. In hindsight, I believe Pappa was too good a gambler to pit the odds of winning against a corrupt-to-the-core government. At the meetings with the attorneys, I saw firsthand how my father's money was being drained away. Nuri would ask my father to come into his private chamber, where he would demand money in cash. When he came out after making a payment, the owners of Sagbara were waiting for their handouts, too. When his funds were almost depleted, Pappa started borrowing money from any source he could find. My father was adamant that because he and his attorneys were right, one day they would win the case.

I was told that my focus was to be on the fruit juice powder factory. I made a couple of trips to the manufacturing site in Pardi. The building was ready for installing the machinery. The next thing on the agenda was to order the machinery for the plant. The Small Business Administration (SBA) loan for a million rupees had already been approved. We had spent our share of equity in the construction of the building. Now it was time to approach the SBA office in Ahmedabad. I gathered the documents and headed to the city, a ten-hour journey by train.

As scheduled, I met with the director at the SBA office. After looking at my documents, he assigned me a loan officer to handle my case. The officer was a middle-aged man with thick glasses. He looked at my file and asked me how much I needed to withdraw. I said about 200,000 rupees to order machinery and for labor charges to install the equipment. He told me that the pro forma we had submitted was old and that it needed to be updated. I had a copy of the old documents in my file. I showed him the file and got instructions on what changes were to be made. The loan officer seemed very helpful, and I left the office feeling happy that for the first trip to Ahmedabad, I had made good progress. I apprised my father of my trip. He was happy that I had made good contact at the SBA office.

That night I sat down at a typewriter to get the five-year financial projection numbers ready, following the guidance of the loan officer. He needed three copies. So I worked out all the numbers by hand and made three carbon copies, burning the midnight oil in the kerosene lamp. This was 1962; electronic calculators and copy machines hadn't been invented. Bill Gates was only seven years old and not thinking about Microsoft Excel just yet. After looking over the numbers carefully, I left the next day for Ahmedabad, very hopeful that I would bring some money home.

After an overnight stay at a hotel, I headed to the SBA office and met the loan officer. He took my file in his hands and fanned through the pages with two fingers. He stopped at some random page and opened the file. He asked me for my name. I said it was Bharat. He put his finger on one number and told me, "Bharatbhai, this number should be changed to number so-and-so. Correct it and then come back." I gently argued that I had done exactly what he had asked for. He told me not to argue and to come back the next day. Instead, I returned to Navapur very disappointed. I reworked the pro forma with a change in the number he had asked for. That meant I had to do all the calculations again—by hand—and retype all three copies.

During my next visit a few days later, the loan officer, the man with the thick glasses, went through the same routine. He fanned the pages, stopped at a random page, and pointed to any number that his finger went to, asking me to change it and then to come back.

The routine continued unchanged for a total of six trips to Ahmedabad. I guess the "cat," my pro forma file, had seven lives. When I made the seventh and the last trip, the officer fanned the pages of the file and threw it on the floor. The file died; the papers, the guts within, flew all over the floor. In a high-pitched, angry voice, he scolded me like I was a stupid child, telling me I didn't understand what was supposed to be done. I had never been treated that way by anyone. I tried to talk, and he told me to shut up, pick up my papers, and get out of his office.

As an inexperienced young man, fresh from college, I didn't know what I was supposed to do. It took me many, many years to figure out the reason for the fanning of my file. The old man was looking for an envelope with 20,000 rupees stuffed in the middle of the file, 10 percent of the requested draw as his commission! How could I know? And if he had only told me upfront, I would have finished the job in no more than two trips. I was back in Navapur with no clue about where I'd gone wrong. One thing I did know: there was no money coming from Gujarat State SBA. I gave a status report to Pappa. With his busy schedule on Sagbara affairs, he asked me to continue the contact with SBA. I knew that was not going to work.

In my own brainstorming session, I thought of contacting large industrial groups to see if they would be interested in equity participation. I wrote a few letters to these companies' headquarters as well as the Maharajas in Gujarat. I did not hear from any of the companies, but one day I was pleasantly surprised to see an envelope with the seal of the Maharaja of Baroda. Inside was a letter inviting me to come and discuss my plan. One morning soon after, I took a train to Baroda. At the palace office, the gentleman who greeted me was none other than Vijay Hajare, a cricket legend, who worked as the Maharaja's investment advisor after his retirement from national cricket. My hands and feet were shaking. He noticed my nervousness and asked me to relax. He poured me a cup of tea, and for a few minutes we talked about cricket. He then asked me to give him a short synopsis of my venture and the size of the investment. Mr. Hajare was impressed with the product line but felt that a one-million-rupee investment was too small for the Maharaja to get involved. I left Baroda at least satisfied that I had tried something different than the SBA and wished the venture was large enough to attract investors like the Maharaja.

Meanwhile, at my age, my family and relatives—except for me—were thinking about getting me married. My cousin Hansa was married and had settled in Surat. One day, while visiting Navapur, after a few days of seeing me around, she mentioned that she knew a girl in Surat who would really be a good match for me. Her name was Surbhi.

This is a classic tale of arranged marriage in India. It teaches you when to hold your cards and when to fold. I told Pappa about Hansa's suggestion. He liked the idea, thinking maybe this was one way to settle me down. He wrote a letter to Surbhi's parents. Upon her return to Surat, Hansa gave my reference to the family. I was invited to visit Surbhi's family. I traveled to Surat and stayed with a relative of ours, Narmadaben. Surbhi's father was Narmadaben's stepson. As I got settled in, Surbhi came supposedly to see her grandma but in reality to meet me. We all sat in the family room and, sneaking a look at each other, we tried to make conversation. Surbhi was a very pretty girl, fair, very sweet voice, with long, braided hair that reminded me of my favorite actress, Sadhna. This would be a great pair, Dev Anand and Sadhna! Soon after Surbhi left, Narmadaben got a call to bring me home in the evening for tea. I had certainly liked her, and apparently she liked me, too. I was very happy and upbeat. So far, I had held my cards all right.

That evening I was escorted to Surbhi's house. I was introduced to her father, uncle, and a couple of menfolk who were part of the interview process. We discussed my studies in Bombay and Mysore, and then the subject got down to the fruit juice powders venture. Meanwhile, the ladies had joined as spectators on the other side of the room. Through a lengthy conversation regarding a choice of final residence and settlement, I surmised that Surbhi's father desired us to settle in Bombay rather than in the small town of Pardi. Once I got the sense of it, I was fully in favor of having a home in Bombay and letting the operations staff run the plant. So far, so good!

Then I had a difficult question thrown at me: What would be my future growth plan beyond fruit juice powders? I had not spent my two years in the CFTRI library for nothing. I gave my verdict with lots of statistics and confidence: the biggest growth that India would experience would be in poultry farming and bottled water for personal consumption. I was asked to clarify poultry farming, which I did. And the final question: "You would enter that business?" With confidence, I said yes! Surbhi's father's jaw dropped with disappointment. Surbhi's maternal grandma left the room, followed by her mother; and then Surbhi, the queen herself, stepped off of the throne. No further questions. The bottom line—Surbhi's father thought that his daughter and this man as her husband, Hindu family members, were going to make living raising chickens. I recognized my blunder. There was no going back to correct anything. I had no choice but to fold the cards; the game was over. No tea was served! I returned to Narmadaben's house in dire disappointment. A week later we received a two-line letter from Surbhi's father. The matter would not be taken any further. I was devastated. I could take harassment from the SBA loan officer or a "no" from the Maharaja of Baroda, but this was personal. For the next couple of days, I just stayed in bed, brooding over the fiasco I had created in my hang-up with chicken.

Pappa watched my behavior for a couple of days, and then he'd had enough. He scolded me and asked me to get out of bed and to get to work. He cautioned me that there would be many more of these kinds of incidents in life; you just can't let that ruin you. Get up and get going! What wise and timely advice. I neither met Surbhi thereafter, nor did I try to make any contact through Hansa. It was a closed chapter in my life. However, the fact remains, as I am writing this chapter, that during the last twenty years, my own town of Navapur has become the poultry capital of India, with many Hindu families making a good living raising chickens along with bottled water as a staple throughout the country. I was simply two decades too early.

By the middle of 1963, I had come to the conclusion that the Pardi factory was not happening. I had no interest in getting involved in the lumber business and did not want to deal with those barristers and attorneys to shell out money that I did not have. I was basically in a rut in Navapur. I did not have any other business ideas, and even if I'd had one, I did not know where the money would come from. The next step was to look for a job in the food industry. Bombay was known for many factories. I made a trip to Bombay and quickly found out that I needed a big-time, inside track referral to even get an interview. I approached a state government food department and sought a job as a food inspector. Getting a job was no problem; they actually needed more people like me. The problem was the salary—three hundred rupees or fifty US dollars per month. What would a man do with that money in a big city like Bombay? The living expenses would be at least ten times the salary. I was then told that the real income would come from the food processors paying me bribes to approve the production plants! I immediately made a U-turn and went back to Navapur.

CHAPTER 5
An Escape Route

I soon approached Pappa with my status report on the Pardi factory. I mentioned what I had read at CFTRI about a country called the United States of America, where the research was done, and that the patent had failed to become a successful commercial process. I told him that in our present financial condition, at least for a couple of years, the Pardi factory would not materialize. I suggested that with his permission, I could go to America to learn the latest techniques of manufacturing fruit juice powders. By that time the Sagbara case would be settled, and we would have our own money to finish the plant. Pappa liked the idea and asked me to proceed further with the plan. I was relieved. He was probably relieved too, as he had realized that my life in India was in a rut and hoped maybe I would find something better in the United States, at least until his own financial condition improved to the point where he could give me a business base in India.

My cousin Lalit was leaving for the United States to study chemical engineering. That gave me a reason to go to Bombay to see him off. I spent a couple of days with him to understand the process of gaining admission to a school, cost of living and tuition fees, travel arrangements, and, most important, getting dollars from the Reserve Bank of India. Lalit advised me to visit the United States Information Service (USIS) in Bombay to get details on universities offering food science and technology degrees.

Many of my friends had left India to study abroad. Satish had left for Germany to study mechanical engineering. Gulab, to my surprise, had also left for the United States to study medical residency. Suresh Joshi, one of my classmates at Wilson College, was at the University of Tennessee at Knoxville, working on a chemical engineering degree.

I applied for admission at US universities that offered degrees in food science. I received many acceptance letters; one was from the University of Tennessee at Knoxville. All of the admissions were for a bachelor's degree, meaning it would take me about three to four years to get the degree. Specialization would take even longer. I didn't care; I had a chance to get out. I sent a letter of acceptance to UT Knoxville and thereafter received details on living and tuition expenses.

During my research at USIS, I had taken notes on important information regarding studying and living in the United States. I learned that the Greyhound bus was the cheapest way to travel; that after a spring semester, a foreign student could work during the summer with permission from a foreign student advisor; and that it would be advisable to bring information on all the courses I had taken in Indian universities that might be helpful in getting credits to avoid repeating any subjects.

The plan was to arrive in the spring and be ready to get a summer job within three months of arrival. I had to raise money for my tickets and one-quarter of my expenses. I believed I could handle the budget that way. I gathered all the material related to the courses I had taken, especially in biological sciences.

I told my friends that I was leaving for the United States to study food science and technology. Word spread in town. Some people were happy and congratulated me; others were skeptical, as my last six years had proven unproductive. I only had a low level Bachelor's degree and had failed in business.

Coming back to the reality of life in those days, the money cabinet at home was almost empty. On one shelf there was a tin box with a few five-rupee notes and some one-rupee notes. I had prepared a budget that included an airline ticket, the cost of travel within the United States to reach Knoxville, and my first quarter's tuition and living expenses. It came to 12,000 rupees, about $2,000. I had decided not to burden Pappa and initiated my own contacts with family and friends to raise the funds.

One day I was passing by Shantamasi's house on Shroff Street. Shantamasi and my mother were the best of friends. As I passed her house, she noticed me and shouted my name. I looked back, and she signaled for me to come to her front porch. She sat down and very quietly asked about my plan to go to the United States and how much money I would need. I told her the amount. She told me that she had 4,000 rupees saved for me; and whenever I was ready, I should come and get it. This was not to be divulged to anybody, not even to my mother.

After a few weeks of knocking on some doors, I finally got a commitment for another 4,000 rupees from one of my father's friends. I was close to reaching my goal and decided to leave for Bombay to make travel arrangements.

Lalit had given me information about a travel agent whom he had engaged for his trip to the United States. One late afternoon I reached the travel agent's office, a big enterprise with a lot of desks and many people talking on the phones with various clients. As I walked down the aisle, I saw everybody was busy. I saw two ladies at the end of the office, sitting at larger desks. They seemed to be supervisors and were not occupied right then. Both of them noticed me walking toward them and greeted me with a smile.

As I walked toward them, I saw them chuckling and possibly deciding which one would handle me. I introduced myself and gave my reason for being there. Both gave me their names. It seems Rita had won the toss; she said with a smile that she would take care of me. Both ladies were pretty and wore beautiful saris. I enjoyed the warm reception from the beautiful women. Rita worked on the plan, and her friend checked flight schedules and connections. March 7, 1964, was picked as the date to leave Bombay by Alitalia airlines, with various stops on the way to New York.

I arrived at Lalit's house that evening. After dinner, Lalit's father asked me about my plans and need for money. He and Pappa were good friends, and he knew the difficulties I might be facing. I gave him the report on my budget and told him I needed to raise 4,000 rupees. Immediately he said that he would have it for me. I thanked him profusely and slept very well that night.

I arrived back in Navapur and told my parents that I would be leaving in a month. News quickly spread all around town that Bharat was leaving for America. I was invited to many homes for dinner and short receptions to congratulate me and to wish me a happy voyage. At every home I was adorned with red *tika*, a red powder dot put on the forehead, for good fortune and was given some rupees to spend on the way. Following Hindu tradition, I accepted the good wishes while bowing down in respect.

My last two weeks at home were getting serious. I was doing some packing in a room behind the living room where Pappa conducted business. A few of his good friends and well-wishers came to see him. Many had the same advice for Pappa: Bharat should get married before he leaves for the United States. The main reason was that the environment in the western world was very tempting, and I might get involved with someone over there. If that happened, my father would lose his son, because he would never want to return home. My father's answer: "If Bharat is convinced that the girl he marries is the right one to belong in Manubhai Diwan's family, she may be from a western world. I have no problem." Then he elaborated: "I don't want to tie him down, and worse, if he decides to marry someone there, I don't want to ruin the life of the girl whom he marries here and leaves her behind." For the first time ever, I understood my responsibility to my family and the faith my father had in my conduct while giving me the freedom to act on my own. That responsibility has remained a guidepost for me ever since.

During those days there were five of us at home: my parents, sister Malini, brother Sanjay, and me. Malini was about twelve years old, and Sanjay was about ten. Saryu and Kunju were already married. One evening Pappa, my mother, and I were sitting at the dining table, discussing my plans before we all left for Bombay. Mother was worried about her son leaving for America, even though he had returned home unscathed after four years in Bombay and two years in Mysore. She asked me to give her a promise. I said, "Go ahead and tell me what you want; I'll do whatever you ask me to." She asked me to promise not to touch alcohol. I was about to agree, but Pappa interrupted. He said the western world's weather gets very cold, and he had heard people drink whiskey and brandy to keep them warm. So if their son needed to take a drink to keep him warm, she shouldn't tie him down with a promise not to touch alcohol. On the other hand, father promised her that when her son Bharat returned from America, he wouldn't be addicted to alcohol; he wouldn't be a drunkard! I was amazed by the trust and open relationship expressed by my parents that night and carried this exchange with me.

Only a few days were left before my departure. I wanted to visit Nareshvar to get blessings from Shri Rang Avdhut, lovingly known as Bapji. I left for Nareshvar with only a backpack and reached the ashram that night. I found out Bapji came out of his cottage around six every morning, and I had to catch the six-thirty bus from Nareshvar to take a train back to Navapur. I had to plan my timing carefully. I got up in the morning, took a bath, and got ready to meet Bapji. At six o'clock I was outside of his cottage, waiting for him to come out. I waited for half an hour, but for some reason he didn't come out. Not wanting to miss the bus, I ran toward the outside gate, convincing myself that I had done my duty. Bapji should know that I was there to see him, and he would have blessed me anyway. So, being outside of his cottage was enough.

The bus arrived. I was the only passenger. The bus driver got down and went to the tea shop. I asked him how long he would be at the shop; he said about ten minutes. I asked him to wait for me because I was leaving my backpack in the bus, and I was going to get Bapji's blessings. The driver said not to worry. I ran toward the cottage, and through the hazy dusk I saw someone sitting in an easy chair outside of the cottage. I knew it had to be him. When I got there, I sat in front of the chair. Bapji was meditating, reciting OM. Every year, all through my college life, I had come to Nareshvar for his blessings. During those visits I never spoke a word. I sat among many devotees and just listened to the conversation. At the end, I would bow down and leave. This moment was different. I was the only one with him. After a while I said, "I'm Manubhai's son from Navapur. I'm leaving for the United States for further studies and have come to ask for your blessings."

Bapji replied, "*Fateh Karo!* Victory to You!"

I bowed, got up, and ran toward the bus. As promised, the driver was waiting. I still carry the vivid memory of the purity of the air at dusk in Nareshvar—the quiet ashram, the birds singing, the peacocks playing on the grounds, and Bapji sitting by himself outside his cottage....

Fateh Karo! Victory to You!

CHAPTER 6
Coming to America

With Parents - Coming to America, 1964

On March 6, 1964, Navapur station was packed with people. Many of the townsfolk had come to see me off. As a part of Hindu tradition, each person brought a garland for me, and I was fully decked. All my friends were coming with me as far as Bombay. Many of my relatives were also joining us all the way to Bombay. Four hours after the train left Navapur, it reached the Surat station. There was a big gathering at the station, as many of my relatives lived there. We were taking a night train to Bombay. We arrived at Lalit's house; and after an evening prayer, we left for the airport. Rita and some of her staff from the travel agency were waiting with my tickets and other documents. The atmosphere at the airport was as if some celebrity was leaving, with garlands, family and friends, photographers, offerings of sweets, and red *tika* for good fortune! Finally, it was time to leave. I bowed to my parents and asked for their blessing. Mother had tears in her eyes. She knew of the financial hardship of the family and why I was leaving. Pappa gave me a hug and pressed a few dollars into my hand, giving me a kind look. I understood his message: "This is all I have." I held back my tears and picked up one garland made of sandalwood petals, given to me by my mother. I waved good-bye to all who took so much trouble to see me off to America. While taking a seat in the plane, I shed a few tears quietly so no one would notice and then composed myself. I realized that from that moment on, I was on my own. I had to be ready to handle any struggle and to meet it head on. Crying wasn't going to help.

After making stops in Rome and Munich, I arrived at London's Heathrow Airport. Chimanbhai, a family friend, was to pick me up. I came out of the airport and, after waiting a while, realized that he was not there. A number of phone calls to his house went unanswered. I took a train to Golders Green, a suburb of London, where he lived. I lugged my two suitcases through the cutting cold. As the train came into an open area, the cold wind got me shivering. I pulled out a golden balaclava from one of the bags and put it over my head and neck. I was in a black suit with a golden cap over my head, which made me look like a monkey. I stood in a corner, watching over my bags. A few girls came aboard at one station. As they settled down and got a glimpse of me, they had a little chuckle. Thereafter, they kept looking at me and laughing. There was a monkey in a suit! I had no choice but to keep it on. At least their evening was passing in fun; mine was not.

I looked for a taxi at the station, and there was none. Golders Green seemed to have a lot of immigrants from India. I met one Indian gentleman outside the station, showed him Chimanbhai's address, and asked for directions. He said the house was about a mile from the station. I took off walking with the bags in my hand, resting along the way whenever my hands and legs got tired. I finally reached the house. I rang the bell and knocked on the door many times. When no one opened the door, I decided to return to the station and find someplace to spend the night. On the way I saw a sign saying "vacancy" at a neighborhood hotel. I went to the desk and asked for a rate.

The white gentleman replied, "There's no room."

I told him about the vacancy sign outside.

He said, "Yeah, but not for you. Find something else." His tone said, "Get lost!"

Exhausted, I headed back to the station. Along the way I met a Sardarji, a Sikh from India. I asked him if there was a place I could spend the night. He gave me directions to India House. He said an old lady named Aajibai, who ran India House, would give me a room. I arrived at India House at about midnight. After listening to my ordeal, Aajibai settled me into a room.

The next morning I made a call to Chimanbhai's house, and, to my surprise, he answered the phone. I told him where I was without giving any details of the night before. He came to pick me up, and we were at his house in no time. Chimanbhai was by himself, as the family was visiting India. He brought up the subject of the night before. Apparently, he had been at the airport, but at the bar, not at the baggage claim. He said he forgot he had come to pick me up and by the time he remembered why he was there, it was already midnight, four hours after my flight had arrived. He was so embarrassed that he ensured my visit to London went quite well after that. He drove me around London in his car where we visited Big Ben, Buckingham Palace, Madam Tussaud's Wax Museum, Trafalgar Square, and other attractions. After spending a day and a half together, I was on my way to New York.

On March 12, 1964, at about two in the afternoon, I arrived at New York's John F. Kennedy Airport. I took a bus to the Greyhound terminal in Manhattan and then on to Baltimore, where Suman Patel, my neighbor in Navapur, was living. He had left India a few years earlier to study and had settled there. By midnight I arrived at the city terminal, and Suman was there to pick me up. The next morning, after Suman left for work, I walked the streets and located a post office. For the rest of that day, I did nothing but write letters to my parents and friends back home. As I was writing with emotions of being lonely in a foreign land, tears rolled from my eyes in a steady stream. I was very careful not to allow a single drop to fall on the paper.

Two days later I headed down to Athens, Ohio, where my cousin Lalit was a student at Ohio University. The bus reached Chillicothe at about five in the morning. We were informed that the bus would not go any further because of the flooded Ohio River. Everybody was asked to gather his or her bags and get further instructions inside the terminal. Keeping my bags in sight, I stood in line to get more information on how to reach Athens. The answer was to wait until the floodwaters subsided so that the bus could cross the bridge. A soldier in uniform was next in line behind me. After he got the same answer, he came and sat next to me. He asked me if I was going to Athens, and I said yes. He said he was going to Columbus, which was a little farther than Athens on the same road. He suggested we take a cab to the highway and wait for somebody to give us a ride. I trusted him and agreed to go along with his plan. I asked him what to do with my two bags. He suggested I take out what I needed and leave the bags in the lockers at the terminal. I took some clothes and some toiletries out in a small bag and left the bus station. We were on the highway, in the middle of nowhere, in heavy rain. This was my third day in America, and I was already hitchhiking! A few cars drove by, but nobody stopped. After about half an hour, a station wagon passed us, stopped, and drove in reverse toward us. We ran to the car.

Someone from inside the car asked, "Officer, where are you heading?"

He replied, "To Columbus, and my buddy wants to go to Athens."

The guy said, "Hop in, gentlemen."

They dropped me off near the campus, and from there I found Lalit's apartment. I knocked on his door, and to both of our pleasure we were together again—in America! I presented him with Lata Mangeshkar's latest record album, and he was very happy. Later we went in his friend's car to Chillicothe and grabbed my bags from the terminal. After two days in Athens and after meeting some of Lalit's friends, I was feeling better. From there I was on my way to Knoxville, Tennessee, where I was to start school in one week. Once I had reached a bus terminal in Knoxville, I took a cab to Suresh Joshi's apartment. Suresh and I had been chemistry classmates at Wilson College, Bombay, and both of us had lived at Mackichan Hall. The real life in America was about to begin.

CHAPTER 7
University of Tennessee, Knoxville, Tennessee

I woke up early the next morning and walked to the main campus at the University of Tennessee. There, I took a bus to the agricultural campus, where the Department of Food Science and Technology was located. I had carried with me my graduation certificates; a list of courses I had taken, with descriptions of the material covered; and a few textbooks we had used at CFTRI, Mysore. Fortunately, the head of the department, Dr. Melvin Johnston, was in his office. I introduced myself as a new student from India. He was happy to see me. I discussed my admission for a bachelor's degree and the courses I had taken during the last six years. I told him that I thought I should qualify as a graduate student. He looked at all my papers and called the dean of graduate study at the main campus, asking if we could see him. We drove to the campus in his car. Dr. Johnston explained the situation of my previous study to the dean, and in less than thirty minutes, I became a master's student, without needing any extra credits. My mission was accomplished.

Within a couple of days, I found an apartment near the main campus and rented a mailbox at the university center. I wrote my first letter from Knoxville to my parents. I wrote that I was happy and not to worry about me. A few days later, I received my first letter in my mailbox. It was from my father—a long one, as usual. He wrote that even though Navapur was going through difficulties, the Sagbara case would soon be over, and he was confident he would win it. He laid out the high expectations he had for me as the pride of the family and said that I had a bright future ahead of me. All those tears I hadn't allowed to fall before were running down my face as I read the letter all the way to my apartment. I read it many times over.

My friend Suresh Joshi's apartment was a gathering place for Gujarati students from India. On one such evening, I met Mahesh Mehta, nicknamed "Mac," from Surat. Mac and I clicked. He was an undergraduate student and had been in Knoxville for a couple of years. Mac knew the ropes in town, and everybody knew him. He owned a big red 1958 Chevy and was familiar with a lot of students' hangouts. One evening we went to Mac's favorite place, the Baptist Student Center. After watching the American kids play Ping-Pong, we asked if we could play. As we played, we were returning low balls from one side to the other, using backhand shots and all the other tricks. Word spread quickly through the three-story building, and the Ping-Pong room was soon packed with people watching the Indians show off their art. We became favorites at the Baptist Student Center. Mac said he had been waiting for two years to find someone like me who enjoyed life!

The spring quarter was about to end. I was pulling a four-point zero average, and Dr. Johnston was happy. However, my money was running low, and it was about time to start finding a job. I received a work permit from the foreign student advisor's office. As I finished my last exam and walked out of the room, Mahesh and five other Indian students picked me up for our journey to Baltimore. A couple of guys in the car had worked there a year before. I did not even know what kind of jobs we were looking for; I had just followed Mac. We rented an apartment, and the landlord was kind and willing to work with us for the rent money. We gave him a small deposit, with the rent to be paid as we found work. The following morning, Mac saw an ad in a local newspaper looking for candidates to sell Bibles. After two days of training, we loaded up Mac's car with Bibles and started our pitch door-to-door. A week later, when the landlord arrived to collect our rent money, we had none to give him. We told him we were selling Bibles, but in five days we hadn't sold a single copy.

He laughed and asked what our holy book was. We said it was the Geeta.

He asked, "If you guys were selling the Geeta door-to-door in India, would anyone buy it?"

We all said no.

He told us that anybody who needed a Bible already had one. Seven guys can't make a living selling Bibles!

Overnight a few from our party left the place and went elsewhere, and soon all the others followed until just Mac and I were left in the apartment.

In a few days we found jobs as dishwashers at an Italian restaurant. Within a week, both of us were promoted to waiters. One evening a pretty girl walked in and was assigned a table I was serving. She ordered spaghetti and meatballs and a salad and said she was on a diet. Wow, that was my field, counting calories! I brought up my food science background and struck up a good conversation. I was having a good time. When my new friend's dish was ready, I grabbed it with gloves, but part of my right hand was still exposed. As I was rushing with my hand burning, I slid the plate on the table. It kept on going and landed on the floor. The spaghetti, meatballs, and red tomato sauce were all over the place, ruining so many dresses and suits. I was so shocked to see what a little mistake created such a mess all over. The owner, an old lady, cursed the hell out of me, pulled off my apron, and fired me on the spot! I was devastated. The hard-earned job was gone in no time. I had had enough of my lonely fight and needed someone who I knew well to give me shelter for a while. Gulab, my friend from Wilson College, was in the United States for his medical residency. He was in McKeesport, Pennsylvania, a suburb of Pittsburgh. I called Gulab; he demanded that I take a bus to McKeesport. By early morning I was there.

For the next couple of days, Gulab took me around to meet a few heads of departments at the hospital. He introduced me as a master's student in food science and said that I was there to spend some time with him. One evening while I was watching TV at Gulab's apartment, he called me. He said Mickey, head of the blood bank at the hospital, had just asked him if I could help her with her chemistry lessons. I had met Mickey the day before at lunch. She was a big, middle-aged German lady. She was taking chemistry classes to maintain her certifications. I rushed to the blood bank and knocked on the door. She took me inside, and we sat at a table in the center of the lab. She showed me her textbook, and it looked familiar. I asked her which topic she had problems with. She showed me a periodic table, very elemental fundamentals, without which everything remains blank in chemistry. I asked her if I could use the blackboard. She helped me to wipe out everything. I started by helping her gain a very basic understanding of elements and then moved on to explain how compounds are formed and how each reaction formula is constructed from the compounds. Within about an hour and a half, I had filled up both the blackboards. She was excited beyond belief; her certification depended on passing this course. She offered me a cup of coffee and asked me how I was enjoying my vacation. I said I was not on vacation; I was actually looking for a summer job. It was about eleven at night. She picked up the phone and dialed a number, and a conversation started: "Mayor, this is Mickey at the blood bank. I have a bright young chemist in my office. He taught me in no time what that son-of-a-bitch at school couldn't teach me in a month and a half. He's saved my life. He's looking for a summer job. Do you have something for him?"

The mayor replied, "Send him to my office at ten in the morning," and hung up.

I did not know what to expect the next morning. A little before 10:00 a.m., I was at the mayor's office. He was a tough guy, ordering everybody around, getting jobs done for the day. As I sat in a corner, he stared at me and asked, "And you are…?" I said I was Mickey's friend from the blood bank. Looking at his assistant, he ordered, "Bill, this is Mickey's friend from the blood bank. Put him to work." I was whisked away to the city's water plant. I did not know what my job was or what my pay would be— and I didn't dare ask. I was assigned a job as a lab technician at the city water department.

Two weeks later, I received my first check. I looked at the amount and couldn't believe my eyes. I was paid for forty hours per week at $7.50 per hour. Minimum wage in 1964 was $1.15 per hour. When I reached the hospital, I showed the check to Gulab. My summer had started very badly, with a lot of missteps, but the end was pleasant and surprisingly rewarding. Only in America!

When I returned to Knoxville, I was probably the richest Indian kid in town. I quickly caught up with Mahesh, and we decided to room together. Living near the campus was important. There were many old homes that had been converted into rooming houses. We started driving and stopped wherever there was a sign outside for rooms to rent. As we were walking up the steps of one large house, we were stopped by two ladies sitting on the front porch, watching us foreigners coming up. One screamed, "What do you want?"

We said, "Ma'am, we want to rent a room."

She replied, "There are no rooms for you guys."

We understood what that meant, and somehow I had no problem with that comment. I had experienced discrimination in Bombay while going to school there, in London trying to rent a room on a cold night, and now this. It was 1964; the civil rights laws were not enacted yet. As a matter of fact, there was a restaurant just outside of campus with a sign on the front that read, "Coloreds and dogs are not allowed."

After getting up the front steps of a few more houses and being told we weren't welcome, we found a kind woman named Louise who rented us rooms. My roommate's name was Bill Ramey, and Mahesh's was a guy named Paul.

I put together a budget covering the completion of my master's degree courses, writing a thesis, and getting it typed. I put away that amount in a savings account, not to be touched. I worked for two hours a day in the school cafeteria, where I got two free meals every day and thus saved on grocery expenses. I was really feeling good about being self-sufficient. I still had a surplus and decided to buy a car, a 1954 Pontiac without radio or AC, for $225 cash! A prodigal son wrote a letter to his father. I announced I was doing great, my grades were the highest in the class, and I had made very good money during the summer. Of course, my proud father spread the news. It soon reached all over Navapur and all my relatives every-where: "Bharat is on the move!"

As the new semester classes began, I met Ashwin, Gulab, and Thakor—all three of them Patels—who had come from Vallabh Vidya Nagar University in Gujarat to pursue master's degrees in food science. Dr. Johnston was especially happy with my academic progress because he had been so instrumental in getting me into graduate school. The Patel boys, on the other hand, had problems. Their level of English was not suf-ficient to carry their course load. I remembered my days at Wilson College, so I spent a lot of time with them, especially on weekends and on the night before an exam, to help them through the hard times. There were many houses near the UT campus where only the Gujarati men shared the rooms. For all of them, I was a weekend driver to get each house filled with groceries. In return, my weekends were filled with Gujarati feasts. Within my Gang of Seven in Navapur, we called each other *Bhidu*, or 'Dear Friend'. Among all Gujaratis in Knoxville, I was known as Bhidu. I felt needed, and I was always willing to help. In return they loved me for my straightforward, upbeat style. And I was always there to console anyone who was worried or depressed. If there was any conflict among roommates, they would call me to discuss the situation. I would remain unbiased, provide my two cents' worth, and leave them smiling at the end. Life seemed worthwhile. I was a happy man.

Mahesh and I lived with about twelve students. We were the only Indians. Our lifestyle with the American students was different. Everyone had their own schedule except we met for morning breakfast. My room had two desks and two beds. When we sat down to study, my roommate, Bill, would invariably bring up a topic to provoke me. Regardless of the topic, we would end up wrestling like brothers. The winner would have won the argument.

Mahesh's roommate, Paul, was a party guy. One Saturday night he invited us to a party. Mahesh, Jerry, and I met Paul and his date, Jane, at their friend's house. There were a lot of people at the party. This was my first outing with American guys and girls. Within an hour Paul got drunk. Jane, Paul's date for the evening, became upset and started crying in another room. As I was passing by the room, I saw her. No one seemed to care. I went to her and asked why she was crying. She said that Paul was very drunk, and she was scared of him when he got like that. Jerry, a two-hundred-fifty pound giant, had already taken Paul to another room and was looking after him. I told Jane to go back to the party and have fun. I told her that I would keep an eye on her so no one would bother her. All through the evening, I remained close to her.

Bharat - College Student

Many times she would put her head on my shoulder and stand with me. This was my first experience of being so close to a girl. Jane was slim, tall, and pretty. I liked the closeness but kept a distance from any move that might seem to take advantage of her. At about 2a.m., the party ended. Jane asked us to take her home. She lived in a small town near Knoxville. Mahesh drove his car; Jane and I sat in the front with him. Jerry sat in the backseat with Paul, who had passed out. When we reached Jane's home, Mahesh and I got out with her. She thanked both of us and pulled me aside. She hugged and kissed me many times and gave me her phone number to keep in touch. This was a new and pleasant experience for a foreign kid on the American scene.

The next morning Paul came to my room and thanked me for taking care of Jane. He told me that he had screwed up the relationship and that it would be all right with him if I wanted to date her. I believe Jane had told him that she wanted to go out with me. A new chapter, however scary, had begun. Jane had a friend named Marla, and Mahesh and I double-dated the girls for a couple of months. One late night, after dropping the girls off at their homes, we were returning to Knoxville. The night was cold, and there was a light drizzle. As we were passing over a bridge, we hit an invisible sheet of ice on the cement road. The car skidded toward a bridge rail, and for the length of the bridge, we slid from one side to the other, hitting the rails on both sides. We could not control the car. I felt that this was it for life in the United States, and death was near! After we crossed the bridge, we were still sliding, and we went off the road and landed in sand on the riverbank. The car was big, and because of the sand, we were saved from a rough landing. Thankfully, Mahesh's AAA membership got us pulled out of the sand. We decided it was too far for us to do a round trip every time we went out with Jane and Marla, and we gradually stopped seeing them. Soon after, we found another pair of friends, Mary and Cathy, on the main campus; and for a while, we dated them.

The spring of 1965 arrived, and I had to get serious about completing my research work, writing my thesis, and preparing for the oral exam. All the dating and going out had to be put on hold. My master's degree in food science and technology was only a start. My goal was to receive training in the fruit juice dehydration process. I sent résumés to many food companies. The Vietnam War had shaken up the US economy, and jobs were hard to find. One of the senior students in the department advised me to apply for a doctoral scholarship. There were better chances of that than of getting a job. I followed his advice and applied to about ten universities. Meanwhile I graduated with a master's degree in food science and technology. Once again, I did not attend a graduation ceremony; job hunting was my main agenda. During the next couple of months, I received two replies out of the two hundred I had sent to various companies. One said I had no experience; the other said I was overqualified. There was no answer from any of the universities. As Chicago was the headquarters for many food companies, I drove there to look for a job. I rented a cheap room on Michigan Avenue. As I had been taught by Guru Mahesh, I found a neighborhood cafeteria and visited it every morning for a cup of coffee. The purpose was to find a waitress who would be kind enough to take phone messages in case a company called for an interview. I eventually got help from Sylvia, the owner of the place. I had a map of the greater Chicago area and located the major food companies. I left résumés at each of them and at some employment agencies. One morning, when I arrived at the coffee shop, Sylvia gave me a message. A personnel director of one company had called, and I was to call him back. When I returned the call, I was told that a processing plant near Saint Louis was looking for a quality control manager. Would I be interested? My answer was yes. I got the address, phone number, and name of the plant manager. I told him that I would be there the next morning.

Saint Louis, Missouri, is about 650 miles from Chicago. I was good at driving at night and could cover 200 miles in three hours. I left Chicago in the evening and was soon covering the distance as planned. The car had no radio, so I was my own entertainer, singing songs on the way. Around five in the morning, I was approaching Saint Louis. It was raining. I was behind a truck and started to overtake it. As I sped along in the left lane at about 90 mph, I saw a road sign for a sharp curve ahead. I passed the truck, and the curve came too soon. As soon as I applied the brakes, the car skidded 180 degrees and went airborne. I landed in a pond on the side of the road. I took out a flashlight from the glove compartment and opened the door. As I got out, I found myself in knee-deep water. The pond was surprisingly deep, which probably saved me, as the car just floated for a few minutes. I saw that I was way down in the ditch from the road. The truck driver had seen my car going down, so he stopped on the side of the road. When he saw my flashlight, he asked if I was all right; I said yes. He said he had seen me flying through the air and had been concerned for my life. He gave me a ride to a gas station a few miles down the road. Fortunately, I had a AAA membership, so the gas station sent a truck to pull the car out of the water and brought it to the gas station. Amazingly, there was no damage. While the mechanic dried out the battery, the carburetor, and other parts, I shaved in the bathroom, changed into a suit and a tie, and got ready to head out to the processing plant for my interview.

Around nine in the morning, I arrived at the plant. It was a chicken processing plant owned by Ralston Purina. The name of the town was California, Missouri, with a population of three thousand! I met the general manager. After a few introductions and questions about my trip, we took a tour of the plant. For the first time in my life, I saw live chickens hanging upside down on a conveyor belt, bleeding and being prepared to be scalded in superheated steam. I believe my master's thesis on the effects of fat on chicken meat had brought me to this plant. As quality control manager, I would check the microbiological quality of the blood, meaning that, all day long, I would be collecting blood samples from the bleeding birds. The other tests were to ensure that the meat was fully cooked. I was given a list of checkpoints about where and how to collect the samples. We finished the tour at about eleven, and the manager offered me a job with a yearly salary of $7,500. I accepted the offer; I needed a job badly and had no choice. He had been looking for someone for quite a while and was happy he had finally filled the position. He offered to take me out for lunch. After returning from lunch, we were discussing the rental options in town, and just then his phone rang. After a moment, much to my surprise, he handed the phone to me. The person at the other end introduced himself as Dr. Salunkhe from Utah State University in Logan, Utah. Then he asked, "Are you the Bharat Shah from University of Tennessee, Knoxville?" I said yes. On the other end of the phone, Dr. Salunkhe offered me a doctoral assistantship and as well as a financial package. With my mind racing, I asked him to repeat the numbers for me to write down. At the end of the call, he gave me his phone number and gave me twenty-four hours to accept the offer or decline. I said I would call within an hour. My method of communication had worked. Barbara, the department secretary in Knoxville, Sylvia, the owner of the cafeteria in Chicago, and I were a triangle grid. I kept up with both of them on a daily basis, and they kept up with each other.

Sitting at his desk, with a bit of an angry expression, the manager was quietly looking at me as I finished writing the numbers. I gave him the news that I was being offered a doctoral scholarship at Utah State University. Then I asked him, "Sir, what would you do if you were in my position?"

He then leaned forward and replied that he'd had a similar offer when he was young and hadn't taken it, which to this day he still regretted. Then he smiled and said, "Son, you go ahead and get your PhD while someone is willing to pay for your education. I will find somebody to fill the position. I wish you the best." With his blessing, I used his phone to call Dr. Salunkhe. I told him I was accepting the offer. He asked me if I could be in his office on Monday morning. I said, "I'll be there!"

It was Friday afternoon. I studied the map and calculated that I had to cover 1,500 miles in only two days. I was going to go through Kansas, then up north to Nebraska, and then into Utah. Ignoring the speed limits, I drove as fast as I could. At two in the morning on Saturday, I was ambushed by cops just outside of North Platte, Nebraska. I was almost put in jail for the weekend. My sincere pleadings, my long name that they could not pronounce, and my books in the trunk convinced them that I was a foreign student and needed mercy. I was asked to drive within the speed limit, at least in Nebraska, and I did!

I reached Logan, Utah, on Sunday afternoon and checked in at the Holiday Inn. After settling down, I called Dr. Salunkhe at his home. He asked me how was my flight? I replied that it was fine. He said, "Welcome to Logan!"

CHAPTER 8
Utah State University, Logan, Utah

Dr. Salunkhe invited me for a dinner at his house that evening. I met Kanu Dalal, another doctorate student from India, at the dinner. Dr. Salunkhe was from Pune, India, and was a research professor at Utah State University. He was known as Chip Salunkhe and was greatly respected on campus. After dinner, I went with Kanu to his apartment. We discussed the research topics available, and he advised me to take the flavors project under Dr. Olson.

Monday morning I met Dr. Salunkhe and Dr. Olson and discussed the various research projects available for the doctoral work. Finally, we decided on a project to identify the differences in flavor components in vine-ripened tomatoes compared to artificially ripened ones. The results of the study had commercial implications for tomato growers in the United States. The selection made me a recipient of a research grant from the prestigious National Institute of Health. Dr. Olson then took me to the lab where other doctoral students were working. There were a total of ten of us: Chan and Chuang from Taiwan, Lee from Korea, a fellow from Japan, Kanu from India, Bart Wenkier from Logan, and two US Army majors, Bill Nabors and Bill Bollings. I began my work in the lab and learned to use some sophisticated equipment. Meanwhile, as the fall semester started, I took some classes to fulfill the credits required for a doctoral degree. The university had a host family program, whereby local families would act as hosts to foreign students. I was assigned the Kindred family, Ted and Betty Kindred, in Hyrum, Utah, a small town about five miles from Logan.

Within a few days I got settled into a student apartment complex, a former WWII army bunker, where many Indian students lived. Altogether there were about 120 Indian students on campus. I made many friends among them, especially with a group of Gujarati students. Soon after classes began, there was an election for the India Students' Association. I went with a few friends and sat in the audience. There were students from all parts of India, mainly Guajarati, Punjabi, and Sikh. As the election process started, a fight erupted onstage between a group of Gujarati and Punjabi students. Each group wanted their member to become president of the association. I watched the scene for a while and then decided to go up onto the stage. I picked up the microphone and asked everyone to please take a seat and to listen to what I had to say. I told them that my name was Bharat Shah and that I was a new student on the campus. The theme of my speech was this: "Outside of this hall, no one cares to know anything about the India Students' Association, much less who its president is. What's more important is that we unite as Indians and show our host community who we are and teach them about the nation that we represent." A Sikh professor was in the audience watching what was going on with the students from his country. He got up and declared, "This man, Bharat Shah, is your new president." No one questioned his statement. Leaders of both the groups came onstage and asked me to be the new president of the association. They put forward a slate of officers representing Gujaratis as well as Punjabis and asked everyone present to approve it. There was no fight, no election. I was the neutral person who unknowingly unified the group.

Bharat - President, India Student Association - 1965

The association had many celebrations during the year, and we invited American professors and their family members to attend Diwali, the Hindu New Year celebrations. My reputation as a leader of a foreign student body grew on campus. I became a de facto advisor to Indian students, whether they were Gujaratis, Punjabis, or Sikhs. Janak Purohit, Anil Dholakia, Ravji Chowdhary, Yash Paul Soi, Arun Budhiraja, and Najam Zainuddin, became my close friends. My 1954 Pontiac was still running and I had put up a sign at the Greyhound bus station for any Indian or Pakistani student needing a ride to the campus to call me. During my years in Logan, every quarter, I would have five to seven new students staying with me when they first arrived on campus. Almost everyone was homesick. I would console them, promising they would be happier soon and telling them to just give it a little time. I would help them select their courses for the first quarter, advising them to keep their load light until they got used to the system. I got them settled in the dorm or apartments outside the campus.

Around Thanksgiving time I received a call from Mr. Ted Kindred, head of my host family in Hyrum, Utah. I and any of my friends who wished to join were invited for Thanksgiving. The Kindred's were a dream family. Mrs. Kindred (Betty) was very active in preparing food. Tim, their son, was about ten years old; Rebecca and Kathy were about eight and six; and a younger sister Jennifer, about four years old. All the children were happy and willing to play with us foreigners. They were very inquisitive of where we all came from. They were aware of other countries around the world. The dinner was sumptuous, and after various desserts, we returned to the dorm. I visited the Kindred family home many times during my stay at Utah State University.

I was so busy with my research work that I didn't realize when Christmas and New Year came and went. Around the second week of January 1966, I received a Happy New Year card from Milan, Kantimama's daughter, in India. This was out of nowhere! Growing up, our two families had been close. Our families had visited each other often, and I had met and played cards with Milan and her sisters many times when I was young. I had gone to Kadod to see Milan's family before coming to the United States. Milan had grown into a very pretty girl indeed. In admiration, I had asked her mother to make sure Milan went to a good college and got a degree. Milan must have taken my comment to heart as she was a college student at the University of Baroda. I had no idea where she could have gotten my address. The greeting card was a pleasant surprise. My reply to the card was immediate and included a veiled suggestion that we develop a long-lasting friendship. While my real hope was different, I thought that a friendship was a good start. My father and Kantimama were the best of friends. Whenever my father visited Kadod, he stayed at Milan's family's home. One night when my father was visiting, and they had already gone to bed, Milan woke her father up. She had brought his medications and remained with him until he took all of them. Pappa was impressed with the daughter's attentiveness and care. When he returned to Navapur, he had described the event to the rest of us and had mentioned that we needed to bring a daughter-in-law of that caring character into the family. I was probably a sophomore at Wilson College at the time, but that event was inscribed in my mind. That was the type of daughter-in-law my parents desired. Now, years later, the same person who had impressed my father had contacted me on her own. Whatever her motive in sending me a plain vanilla "Happy New Year" card may have been, I wanted to build on that beginning to reach to a different level.

Upon receiving my letter, Milan did not know how to handle its content. She knew and understood very well what it all meant, veiled or not. Manju, her roommate, was a couple of years older and wiser. She read my letter and advised Milan to reply in kind. Milan did not want to move so fast and decided to wait a while before replying. At my end, I was waiting anxiously. I gave up on it when there was no letter for quite some time. One day, there it was, sitting in my open mailbox in the department office. A new journey had begun! From that point on, the exchange of letters continued almost on a weekly basis. As time went on, the contents of the letters became more personal, leading toward a love affair. The letters contained love songs from the yesteryears of Indian cinema. Within a year or so, we were discussing marriage and children—at least twelve we said!

I had spent almost a year on campus. I continued my research work through the summer of 1966 while other students had left for summer work. As the fall semester began, my friends started coming back. One morning, while crossing a street on campus, I saw Yash Paul Soi. Yash was my vice president at India Students' Association. He looked very pale and seemed like he had lost a lot of weight. I asked him if he was OK and why he looked so weak. He said he had worked on an orange farm in California during the summer, and it was very hard work. I felt that there was something serious and insisted that I take him to a student infirmary. There the doctors checked him. They asked me if I was related to him; I said I was a friend. The doctors gave me a note to take to a hospital in Salt Lake City, about ninety miles from Logan, for a further checkup. Yash and I drove to the hospital, and he went through extensive testing. They found that he had a big tumor in the groin. Yash was admitted in the hospital to await the results of the biopsy. By evening, I had returned to Logan and informed the other Indian students. Every evening after classes were over, six or seven of us would jump in my car and go visit Yash in the hospital. One day he was operated on, and the tumor was removed. Fortunately, it was found to be benign.

After about two weeks in the hospital, Yash was about to be released. One evening, when I went to pick him up, the hospital administrator stopped me and asked me to join him in his office. He explained to me that I had brought Yash to the hospital for treatment and had signed certain papers. My signature on the papers meant that I would be responsible for the bill. He informed me that I would have to arrange for the payment before Yash could be released from the hospital. I looked at the bill, and my legs went weak. The total was somewhere around $36,000! I got the copy of the bill and went to see Yash in the room. He knew of the bill situation and also knew that he would not be leaving the hospital that evening. He asked me, "Dada (Big Brother), what are we going to do?" I told him I would go back to Logan and see if I could bring some help. I called Mr. Kindred that night. He asked me to bring the bill to him, and he would see what he could do. The next morning I went to his house in Hyrum. He looked at the bill and very calmly wrote a note to the hospital administrator. Mr. Kindred was a Catholic and maintained a very high position within the church hierarchy. Fortunately, the hospital where Yash was treated was a Catholic hospital. I headed to Salt Lake City from Hyrum and handed over the note to the administrator. He looked at the note and told me that I had very high-level contacts. Then he asked me very kindly to help Yash pack his bag. He then met us in the room and asked Yash to sign a paper, which described the terms of release. Yash was agreeing to pay whatever he could pay whenever he could pay it. Yash gave me a big hug, and we returned to Logan. I kept Yash at my apartment until he recovered fully. We worked very closely as officers of India Students Association.

Sometime during the fall of 1966, Najam Zaimuddin, a student from Surat, India, became my roommate. Mr. and Mrs. Wayman in Logan were Najam's host family. The Waymans were Mormon. As they lived in town, we were invited quite often to their house, on church picnics, and on over-night visits to Salt Lake City to attend Sunday services at the Mormon Tabernacle. I became quite close to Mr. Wayman. He called me Bartley, and our relationship grew to be like a father and son.

In my letters to Milan, I had expressed my desire that we get engaged and that she should come to Utah State, so we could go to school together. She had liked the idea and was to talk to her parents. Meanwhile, my 1954 Pontiac was showing signs of wearing out. I would have to have a good car if Milan were to join me. One day I mentioned to Mr. Wyman that I was looking to find a better car, giving the valid reason of my fiancée ar-riving in town. Bill Wayman was a vice president at Pioneer National Bank in Logan, and he said he would get in touch with me soon. One afternoon he asked me to come to the bank, and he showed me a car. It was a repos-sessed 1962 black Corvair with red bucket seats. I loved it. Mr. Wayman asked me, "Can you afford forty dollars per month in payment?"

"I sure can, Mr. Wayman," I said with a big smile.

"The car is yours, then. Just sign here."

I walked away with a great looking car with a price tag of only $650.

One Sunday the Gujarati guys were preparing a big meal at Janak Purohit's apartment. Janak gave all of us some papers to fill out. I did not know what they were, but I filled them out anyway. Thereafter, when called upon, the group made a few trips to the immigration office in Salt

63

Lake City for a personal interview and for fingerprinting. One day I received a card in a yellow envelope. Unknown to me, as a graduate student, I had applied for immigrant status, and the card granted me just that. At that point I had no idea of its importance and simply tossed it into the desk drawer.

My study and research continued at a normal pace. With ten doctoral students and only one set of equipment, the process to use the equipment was hectic. One day I was late signing up and was the last one in line to use gas chromatogram, an instrument that detects individual flavor components in a concentrate. My assigned time was at 8:00 p.m. I dreaded it and hated the idea of working late at night. The work environment at night proved to be an eye-opener—I was the only one in the lab. Everything was quiet. All the equipments were available without any interference. At the end of my workday, at about 4:00 a.m., I had beautiful graphical results. I was very happy and decided to put my name on the list starting at 8:00 p.m. every night. I would work from eight at night to six in the morning. On the way to my apartment, I would stop at a restaurant just outside of campus and order scrambled eggs, toast, and orange juice. Every morning it was the same place, same table, same menu, and same waitress. From there I would go to the apartment, go to sleep, wake up at about two in the afternoon, get ready, and go to the library to study. The routine was working for me, and I was making real progress in research work.

One afternoon, when I stopped by the lab, Dr. Salunkhe saw me. As I picked up a couple of books from my desk and was about to leave, he stopped me. He was very angry and scolded me, asking me how many girlfriends I had and if I was enjoying the bachelor life in America. In total surprise I asked him why he was asking me those questions. He said neither he nor Dr. Olson or for that matter, anyone in the students' group, had seen me for almost three months. I replied that I was working at nights and was spending the rest of my time in the library. He asked me to bring my work to his office, and I picked up my files and followed him. I had all my charts dated and documented. I had made substantial progress in identifying the differences in flavor components between vine-ripened tomatoes and those that were artificially ripened. As he reviewed my work, his mouth fell wide open.. He apologized for his harsh remarks and called

Dr. Olson to arrange for a meeting with all the doctoral students the next morning at eight. Dr. Salunkhe made a presentation of my work and declared that even though I was the most recent candidate in the group, my progress had surpassed everybody else's. My reputation as a serious research fellow in the department had been recognized. Thereafter, other doctoral students sought my advice in creating a better format for their work. Dr. Olson, who had very rarely spoken to me in a warm or friendly manner, was now all smiles whenever I met him for a discussion of my research work. I was becoming a research scientist.

Kanu Dalal, who had given me advice on selecting a research project, had moved on to University of California, Davis, for a fellowship in food science. During the summer of 1966, I took a bus to San Francisco and arrived there at midnight. At Kanu's recommendation, I stayed at a nearby motel that turned out to be owned by an Indian. Much to my disappointment, the experience was horrible—I found no bathroom in the room, naked guys were walking in the hallway, and I could not lock the door. I was scared for my life—and for the hard-earned two hundred dollars I carried with me. I put up a chair against the door and dozed off while I could, waking up throughout the night. At dusk I called Kanu to get me out of this terrible place. I remember thinking that I would never again have anything to do with Indian-owned motels.

The Davis campus was very large compared to the Utah State campus at Logan. Both were very beautiful. Kanu took me around the campus and showed me the food science department; and after spending a day touring the city of San Francisco, I returned to Logan.

During that summer, Gulab and his wife, Anu, visited Logan with some friends on their way to the Grand Canyon. I had planned to go with them for a tour and had written to my parents about my plan. Within a week after leaving Logan, the car the group was in was involved in a head-on collision. Everyone except Gulab and Anu were killed. The news reached India, and my parents saw it in detail in a local newspaper. The atmosphere at my home was gloomy, because they believed I had been in the group. International communication by phone was non-existent during those times. My parents could not contact me. However, two days later, they received my letter, describing Gulab and his friends' visit and staying at my apartment. And because I was busy with my research, I had decided not to join the group. The family breathed a collective sigh of relief.

During the Christmas vacation of 1967, a few of us decided to go to California to see the Rose Parade. After a couple of days in Las Vegas, we arrived in Pasadena at 9p.m. on December 31 to watch the parade the next morning. The five-mile Colorado Boulevard in Pasadena was packed with people. Finally we found a corner at a crossroads, spread out our blankets, and settled down. We played three-card poker all night long, and a couple of us took turns bringing food and drinks from nearby stores. Whenever I took a stroll, I would go to a drugstore a few blocks away and buy a "Happy New Year" card. I would stamp it and mail it to Milan in India. During the night I sent three Happy New Year cards. Naturally, all the cards reached Milan on the same day. I had no idea that Milan's dorm did not have individual mailboxes; all the incoming mail was hung on a bulletin board. My cards were open, without any envelopes. Milan was embarrassed as everyone who saw a card on the bulletin board, one at a time, came to tell her that there was a card for her. She will run downstairs, pick up the card and in no time there will another card hanging on the board. It was a feast of "love" for every girl to read. Open love letters from America - three in one day no less! Milan became the talk of the dorm, and of course the girls spread the word on campus. Milan was one of the most beautiful girls on the campus. As she would pass by the boys' dorm, someone would whistle, and the other boys would rush to the balcony to watch her. Word spread quickly that Milan had a boyfriend in America and that he was working on his doctorate. Being in America was a lifetime dream of all the guys on the campus. Unknown to me, I had defeated the competition. Little did they know I was not in dreamland. Milan's boyfriend was struggling. Life was tough.

The Vietnam War was at its peak. I did not know or understand the effects of war on the general economy. It had to be bad, because President Lyndon Johnson cut off the National Institute of Health research funds. My assistantship of $350 per month was taken away. I had saved about two thousand dollars for writing my final thesis, and that savings was going down to zero. My plan was to complete my research work, get the thesis printed and approved, and get my doctoral degree. The job market being even worse than in 1965, I had no plans to look for a job. I was homesick and anxious to reunite with Milan. I did not know or care what would happen next.

CHAPTER 9
Homesick, Homebound

Around March of 1968, I received a letter from Milan. The content of the letter was scary. She was about to complete her studies at the University of Baroda with a BA in psychology, and within a couple of weeks, she would be home in Kadod. Her parents were preparing to get her married. There were a couple of suitors; one boy's family was in Bombay, and the other boy was arriving from London. Both were from her Jain community, and both of their families were very wealthy. Milan wrote that unless I came up with a plan, she may not be able to stop the train once it left Kadod. The families knew Milan and were very anxious to have her as their daughter-in-law. If one of the boys likes her, most probably both will like her, then the family of choice from Milan's side will move fast for an engagement ceremony.

I thought all afternoon and decided to write three letters that night. The first one went to her parents. I reminded them of our long family friendship, even though I was not from the Jain community. I expressed that Milan and I were in love and that I was asking for their permission to marry her and promised my commitment to take care of her. I suggested they contact my parents directly in Navapur and not to go through any intermediary. The second letter went to my parents. I expressed the situation in detail, asking for their approval and for them to contact Milan's parents directly. The third letter went to Milan with details of both letters, with a warning to be ready for a harsh reception when she reached Kadod. When she reached home, no one talked about my letter. Her brother told her that they had received a letter from America, and it was in the safe. Milan got hold of my letter, read it, and put it back.

There was some resistance to the relationship from both families—though much stronger in Milan's family than in mine. Milan's mother and paternal grandfather were the most opposed. I understood the situation very well. First, I was a Vaishnav Hindu, whereas Milan was a Jain. We worshipped Lord Krishna; Jains, on the other hand, worshipped Lord Adinath and Mahavir Swami. As much as there were similarities in the religious lifestyles, plenty of ill feeling and discrimination existed among the orthodox families. In Milan's family, the elders of the 1960s era took the difference seriously, however little it was. Second, and most important, Milan's other suitors were from very prominent Jain families. On the other hand, my family was heavily in debt, almost at the brink of bankruptcy. Legal trouble with the Sagbara Jungle had taken its toll, and Milan's family was very much aware of it. In principle, and in practical terms, Milan's mother and grandfathers stance was valid. The resistance at my home was minor. The notion was that I should meet other girls upon my return rather than just pursue this relationship. However, my father was firm in his position. He stopped any further discussion in our family and stated that we would welcome Milan into our family as Laxmi, goddess of wealth and prosperity.

After a few days of arguments, one evening Milan convinced her father that the family members were choosing only financial stability, whereas she was choosing her heart, and that she loved me very much. Her father, whom I also addressed as Kantimama, loved me as much as she did. That same evening, my father called Milan's house. Both of the friends stated that each was waiting for a phone call from the other end. The date for our engagement was fixed, and Milan and I got engaged—myself in absentia. Only in India! I announced my engagement to my friends in Logan, the Kindred and Wayman families. I sat down with Dr. Olson to review the status of my research work. He asked for the remaining data to be worked on, and I pursued that goal seriously. The course work had been completed; so, in just a matter of months, my doctoral work would be at an end.

Mentally, I made plans to return to India as soon as possible. This time I was not going to look for a job; the situation had not changed for the job market anyway. I was running low on money. I had only enough to get my thesis printed, nothing more. I made up a budget for a trip to India and contemplated the ways of raising the money. My only resource seemed to be Mr. Wayman. I called him at the Pioneer National Bank and asked to see him. I presented my numbers. I needed around $5,000 as a personal loan. He asked me if I could get a job letter from my department head and any other collateral that I could put toward the loan. I sometimes taught Dr. Salunkhe's classes whenever he was out of town for seminars and conventions and was his students' favorite substitute teacher. He had offered me an assistant professorship at the university, but at the time I had told him I was interested in an industrial position, especially to get experience in fruit juice powder manufacturing. However, now I remembered Dr. Salunkhe's offer of an assistant professorship, so I went to see him and explained the need for a job offer letter. He gladly gave me one with a request to come back to Utah State if I didn't get a job in the industry upon my return from India.

Furthermore, Ravji Chowdhri had become a good friend, and I asked him for help. He offered his Volkswagen as collateral. My Corvair and his Volkswagen along with the job letter from Dr. Salunkhe became my package to present to Mr. Bill Wayman. He reviewed the package and felt it was appropriate to present to his loan committee. He asked me to contact him when I was ready.

My research work was almost complete by June 1968. I started getting the thesis printed one chapter at a time for review by Dr. Olson. July 15 was the date set for my final examination. On that morning, Dr. Salunkhe, Dr. Olson, and three other professors sat to review my work. As the interview began, Dr. Olson asked me to explain various phases of my research and conclusions I had drawn from the results. The room had two blackboards. As if the professors were my students, I filled up the blackboards with various formulas and answered each question thoroughly. Periodically the group would ask me to step outside so they could discuss whether anyone had any more questions. After a few minutes, one of them would come out, address me as Mr. Shah, and ask me to step in. There would be some more questions and explanations, and I would be asked to step outside again. Finally, after about six rounds, Dr. Olson came out and said, "Congratulations, Dr. Shah; please come in." It sounded just wonderful! Four hours of grilling finally ended with very heartwarming words. I shook hands with everyone, thanked them from the bottom of my heart, and left the room.

I did not go anywhere to announce my doctoral graduation; instead, I got into my car and rushed to a travel agent's office. I asked for a round trip flight from Salt Lake City to Bombay and back. The travel agent informed me that unless I had an immigration green card, I could not get a round trip ticket. I asked, "What's a green card?"

He explained that although they called it a green card, it was actually light blue in color. I remembered receiving a brown envelope from Immigration and Naturalization Service that I had casually thrown into the center drawer of my desk. I rushed to the apartment and found the envelope in the pile of junk in the drawer. The card looked blue, and I prayed that it was what I needed. I rushed back and showed the travel agent my card. "That's it." he said. I thanked my friends, especially Janak Purohit, for bringing the papers to fill out and making sure we all followed the process.

My next stop was at Pioneer National Bank. Mr. Wayman mentioned that the loan committee would approve the loan with my package along with his personal guarantee. He said, without any hesitation or promise in return from me, that he had given a guarantee on the loan. He also mentioned that the bank president had cautioned him that the foreign student might not come back and that Mr. Wayman would be responsible for the $5,000. He had told the president that he was not worried, that "Bartley will come back and pay." I put away $1,000 in a savings account at the bank, spent about $1,200 for the airline ticket, and carried the rest in cash and traveler's checks. I had a farewell meeting with the Kindreds and Waymans, and then I was ready to leave Logan.

Both the families in India were informed by telegram of when I would be arriving at the Bombay airport. I stored my books, a tape recorder, and some tapes in the trunk of the Corvair and left it in the Kindreds' garage. I landed at the Bombay airport on the morning of July 25, 1968. My heart was pumping with excitement to meet Milan, and I longed to see my family, especially my father. As I came up the steps of the Bombay airport terminal, Milan was standing there, waiting for me, with a bouquet of flowers in her hands. She wore a sari and had gotten her hair specially groomed for the occasion. She was absolutely beautiful and had a great smile. I was completely knocked out at the mere sight of her. As I came close to her, I gave her a kiss on the forehead and then a good smooch right on the lips. I had forgotten that now I was in India! All these things happened spontaneously, without any forethought or preparation. What I had missed seeing was that the entire airport was filled with my friends, family, and relatives from both sides and, surprisingly, townsfolk from Navapur. I realized that I had shocked everybody by kissing Milan on the lips but hoped that they would forgive me—after all, I was returning from America and meeting my fiancée for the first time!

Next I noticed my mother. I bowed to her, told her that I was back, and inquired of her health. I moved on, as my eyes were searching for my father. I saw him standing with the other menfolk. As I walked toward him, with my heart so heavy, I let out a loud cry, tears flowing like a stream. I composed myself as I approached him and bowed to everyone standing with him. Milan and I left the airport with my cousin Chandrakant in his car. I was recounting some of my adventures. Quite often as I would forget the names and things I was talking about, Milan would fill in the missing links. I wondered how she knew all these things. It seemed like she was already carrying half of my brain. We would look at each other and exchange a smile. I loved this girl whom I was with now after almost three years of writing love letters. We got settled at Chandrakant's house. I had missed Indian masala tea during my stay in America. Anytime anyone asked me if I wanted to drink anything, it was nothing but tea, even at night. Every time I opened my bag to pull out a gift for someone, my sisters would surround me to see what else I was keeping in the bag.

The first night, Milan and I huddled in a corner of a room and talked until the wee hours of the morning. When everybody woke up in the morning, we also woke up from our individually assigned beds. That afternoon we decided to leave the place and go shopping. I had missed my banjo and decided to go to a music shop that I was familiar with. The shopping area was on a narrow street, with the shops on a second floor. As Milan and I were getting out of the cab and taking the steps up to the shop, someone across the street shouted, "Hey, Sharmila Tagore!" I did not know whether Milan heard the comment or not, but I heard it loud and clear. Sharmila was a very pretty Indian cinema actress, a top heroine of that era. Milan very much resembled Sharmila with her style of wearing a sari and the way she wore her hair. My eyes kept on moving like a secret service agent. Within no time I realized that the crowd on the street was building up. The word was out that Sharmila had come to shop at a musical instrument store. The shopkeeper showed me a couple of banjos, and I abruptly told him that we would return back tomorrow. Milan asked me what happened, and I just answered that we had to leave. Fortunately the cab we had arrived in was still there. I asked Milan to jump in first from the better-protected side, and then I jumped in and asked the driver to rush us back to the same place where he had picked us up. I realized for the first time that I had escorted someone very pretty, and life was going to be a lot more interesting going forward. I was engaged to this beautiful queen and I would be married to her soon!

In the evening, Milan's mother, Ushaba, pulled me to a corner. She asked me about my plan to get married. She asked me if I wanted to just register our marriage or if I wished to go through the religious process. Hindu traditions dictate that the wedding ceremony be conducted at the bride's house. I answered that it would be at her home, following Jain traditions and not necessarily our Vaishnav system. Then she became more direct in her questioning: Did I want to just register the marriage and save expenses, or did I want an elaborate wedding ceremony, which would be quite expensive? I said, "Why do you ask?" She replied that my father wished to just register the marriage. I now understood the reasons for her questions. Then I asked her if she knew what my mother's wishes were, and Ushaba said that my mother wanted the religious process. I understood the scenario and asked her to wait for my answer at a later date.

The next day we all left for Surat by train on our way to my hometown, Navapur. Again there was a big reception at the Surat station. It was a proud moment for the community that one of their own had returned with a doctorate degree from America. More importantly, I was humble in my conversation, approached elders with respect and had no ego of a US returned scientist. I had learned humility and had maintained a good command over our language, Gujarati. From Surat we boarded a midnight train for the five-hour journey to Navapur. Because of the time difference between Utah and India, I was awake; everybody else was sleeping. About an hour before reaching Navapur, the terrain really changed into lush greenery, with mountains in the background. I got up very slowly and went toward the exit door. As I leaned toward the window, someone tapped me on the back. I turned around, and it was my older sister, Saryu. After some casual conversation, she asked whether I burned incense or not. I said, "I do when I pray." She said she was not talking about the prayer incense; she wanted to know whether I smoked cigarettes or not. I replied I did not. Her next question was whether I drank liquor or not. I said, "No! Why do you ask?" She said, pointing to my mother, that mother had a suitcase full of liquor for me. I was shocked! Saryu told me that someone else from our community had returned from studying abroad, and he could not move without having a drink and that my parents had watched him in sheer shock. They had wondered, if a straight kid could get so hooked on alcohol, what would Bharat be like when he returned? Bharat was an all-rounder, full of shenanigans when he left India. Saryu mentioned that all the family members had been watching my movements during our stay in Bombay, and every time I opened my suitcase, they surrounded me, looking for telltale signs of a hidden bottle. Mother had come to Bombay well prepared with cash. She had contacted my cousin Chandrakant to buy foreign imported liquor at any cost. She did not want her son to get sick if he ended up drinking cheap local liquor. That was the height of motherly love, and it remained inscribed in my heart forever. Mother's love knows no bounds, its timeless and endless. Four years prior, this was the lady who had asked me to promise her that I would not touch alcohol. Today she was carrying illegal cargo under her arm so that her son would not get sick. Tears streamed from my eyes. Saryu cried with me, too, but her tears were of happiness that her brother had returned back a better person whom the family could be proud of.

CHAPTER 10
Wedding and Honeymoon

We reached Navapur around six in the morning. Milan had accompanied us, too. Townsfolk poured into our house to see me. After tea and a few words of congratulations and best wishes, one after another, they left. I wanted some time to talk to my father. When I knew all was clear and felt he was at ease, I asked him to set the wedding date. Soon, I saw a very serious look on his face. He said, "I will look for an auspicious day in an almanac, but because of lack of funds, we will do a simple registration process." I asked him what would be my mother's desire. In a very serious tone, he said, "Since you are the eldest son, her desire of course would be to invite friends and relatives and to do a traditional ceremony, but that would be very expensive." I told him that I had brought some funds with me and that we should plan for a traditional wedding and invite a limited number of people. His eyes just sparkled. "You do have money?" I said yes. I still remember the smile on his face and his sense of relief and happiness. His reputation was at stake, and I had come prepared to support his as he had always been there to support mine. Internally, I was also thanking Bill Wayman and Ravji Chowdhri for making it feasible for me. The date was fixed for August 18. My father went to the kitchen and announced to all the ladies present, "Start making preparations for a wedding!" I stood right behind him and was delighted by the elated expression on my mother's face. She was like a baby getting her first toy. She hugged me, and it was probably the best exchange of gifts a mother and son could have. The atmosphere in the house turned festive. Father and I sat down and made a budget for a small wedding that I could financially handle myself.

A few days later, Milan and I left for Kadod, her hometown. We announced the wedding date and our plans for a traditional wedding. Both of her parents were happy with the news. Just as I remembered from my childhood, Milan's home always had a festive air. There were a lot of visitors, and her mother would have plenty of food to offer them. Dinner at Milan's home was usually on floor mats. Milan's father, Kantimama, would sit next to her mother, Ushaba, and serve Milan and me various dishes, which we ate from one large plate. Ever since that time, we have always eaten from one plate.

After a couple of days, I felt like I should return to Navapur. I was certain my mother was missing me, especially as she was making the arrangements for the wedding. However, I was so attached to the new environment in Kadod—and especially spending time with Milan—that I kept on extending my stay. One day Milan's father arranged for a musical evening and invited a few local artists. These guys happened to be my childhood buddies I had played with every summer when I visited my grandparents in Kadod. After a few rounds of songs, someone suggested that the son-in-law should sing. I was just waiting for the opportunity. I could see the smile on Kantimama's face as I started a deep-voiced love song in Hindi with lyrics, "*Marna teri galime, Jina teri galime*", that said, "I would live on your street; I would die on your street; you (Milan) and the townsfolk would remember me for that." I had learned the song from my friend Yash in Logan. I could carry the high pitch very well. It was indeed a memorable evening. I had established my name one more time in Kadod! Finally, just about three days before our wedding day, I returned to Navapur. Friends and family members were waiting. Religious rituals of "Pithi" and "Peace in the House" were conducted to ensure a happy life for Milan and me. My mother, aunts, sisters, and sisters-in-law were having a joyous time. My brother Sanjay was getting ready for his big brother's wedding.

On the morning of August 18, we took a train to Kadod. There were thirty-five people in the wedding party, which included my immediate family, close relatives, and friends. We arrived at my grandparents' house, and within an hour, the procession to Milan's house began. The groom walked too—no horse, no music band, and no extra fanfare as we had a tight budget to follow. The wedding ceremony was done well, and everybody enjoyed the feast that was prepared by chefs specially invited from Surat. Milan and I were so exhausted that we could hardly eat. As usual, photographs were taken with family and friends. A beautiful Jain temple sits across from Milan's house in Kadod, and Kantimama had made a pledge for a prayer by the newlyweds. As Milan and I were going up the temple steps, I saw a lot of people, men and women, who belonged to my religion, watching a Vaishnav boy going to do prayers in a Jain temple. It was unthinkable in those days. I looked at them and smiled. Frankly, I couldn't have cared less. I had no idea that deep down, there would be so much discrimination between the followers of Hinduism and Jainism. Later on I found out that whenever Milan visited Navapur after our engagement; she had experienced some form of discrimination, if not outright blatant mistreatment, from some of my relatives. My younger brother Sanjay was an ardent protector of his Bhabhi, sister-in-law, and my father had stopped all the bickering about it between family members and close relatives. I wondered what was in me, or what faith she had in me, that she had decided to hang on to our relationship and not call it quits. She was educated and very pretty, and well-to-do families were asking for her hand in marriage for their sons. Milan basically didn't know me until I arrived back in India. I was not particularly handsome, either. When Milan and I were together at my grandma's house in Kadod, the old lady praised Milan for her beauty and poise. On the other hand, she scolded me for how ugly I looked, with my thin body and acne all over my face. Later in the evening of our wedding day, we all took a train back to Navapur and arrived at my home. My parents had vacated their bedroom, which became our honeymoon suite. After a few days of parties and picnics, we left for Kadod. We stayed there for a couple more days before leaving on our honeymoon trip.

Nareshvar was our first stop in order to receive blessings from Shri Rang Avdhut. We were told that he had gone to Kapadvanj. We traveled to the town by bus and arrived at the house where Bapji was staying. The host took us to the room where Bapji was in meditation with his eyes closed. When he looked up, I introduced myself and said we had just gotten married and had come for his blessings. Very kindly he said, "Sukhi Raho", "Be happy". We bowed together and left the room. At my mother's request, the next stop was at Shri Nathji, an abode of Lord Krishna, an important beginning point of a pilgrimage for a Vaishnav. After staying overnight, we went to the temple at five in the morning. As the sanctum door opened, we had a graceful sighting of Shri Nathji. The prayer at dawn is known as "Mangala," the most auspicious prayer of the day. My heart was moved. Next we arrived at a town called Ambaji, named after Amba, the goddess of strength, protection, and good fortune. Milan's family followed her. We checked into a room and went to the temple that evening and attended an Aarti, a recitation of prayers with lighted lamps in hand.

Bharat & Milan Wedding Photo

Bharat - Milan Wedding

After all the blessings from Lord Krishna and Goddess Amba, the real honeymoon began. The next evening we arrived at a mountain resort, Mount Abu, and checked into a hotel before going out sightseeing. I had been to Abu before on my school trips, so I knew the whereabouts of various attractions. We spent the evening at a beautiful site, Naki Lake, under a full moon. After dinner at a nearby restaurant, we arrived back at the hotel. We went to our room, changed into our pajamas, and turned the lights out. In a few minutes I got out of the bed; my whole body was itching. As I turned the lights on, I saw hundreds of bedbugs that had decided to share our honeymoon bed with us. Milan and I took the pillows and slept on the floor. The next morning as we were leaving the room, Milan asked me if I had remembered to take my wallet and money from the desk drawer. I had not! That was the beginning of a new chapter in our married life, her keeping an eye on my forgetfulness.

As a last-minute thought, we decided to go to the city of Mysore, where I had received my diploma in food technology. We flew to Bangalore and took a train to Mysore, considering this trip an extension of our honeymoon. There we took a room at my favorite Dasa Prakasha Hotel. I took Milan to the institute and my dormitory where I had stayed for two years. We visited all the attractions of the city, including Mysore Palace. Our favorite was the Vrindavan Gardens, the most exotic place of the time, with beautiful flower beds and decorated dancing water fountains. We found a spot under a tree where nobody would notice us newlyweds, acting like lovebirds as never before, matching our lush, exciting surroundings.

Finally, we returned back to Kadod via Bombay. When we reached Milan's home, the atmosphere was gloomy, and we were concerned. Milan's mother scolded us for not writing a single letter in the two or three weeks we had been gone. Depressed and keeping to himself, Milan's father had quit eating his favorite foods and stopped shaving. When someone informed him that we were home, he came down to see us. He took Milan and me in his arms and shed a few tears. The only thing he said was that he missed us a lot and that we should have written of our whereabouts. Even today, I remember the love and affection he had for us. It was very special!

At my home in Navapur, the family financial situation was dire. Pappa had won the Sagbara case in the lower court; however, the government of Gujarat had appealed the case at the state's high court. The SBA loan for the new factory was still in limbo. One day, during my stay in Navapur, without referring to the family's financial problems, I had talked to my father about life in the United States. I discussed my desire to return back to the States and spend some time there with Milan. He was impressed with my description of life in the United States and agreed that Milan should spend some time there, too. As the circumstances at home had deteriorated even further than four years back, he felt that it was the best plan. Milan was very close to her family and did not want to leave India for a long period. I promised her that we would go to the States for a year and then return to India. I just wanted her to experience the new country I had fallen in love with. She agreed, and we started the process to get her immigration visa at the US Consulate in Bombay.

At the consulate office, the attending clerk was not particularly co-operative, and I understood the reason. I needed to grease his hands. I talked to him about life in the United States, the easy availability of all the conveniences and gadgets that were luxuries in India, and so on. The clerk mentioned having a tape recorder but not having a spare spool of tape. I told him that on my next visit, I would have two for him. He immediately filled out all the forms on our behalf, and we were out in thirty minutes. Approval for a US immigration visa required thorough medical exams and a certification of clearance from a designated medical doctor. After a month of frequent visits to Bombay for various tests, we figured out that we were in a trap orchestrated by the circuit of medical doctors. A friend of my father, an insurance agent, pulled us out and helped us to get the required certification. With approval papers in hand, we went to the con-sulate's office. Our clerk friend, who had already been given two spools of tape during one of our earlier visits to Bombay, saw us and came running to greet us. He said the consul himself wanted to see us. The chief's office was impressive, with a ceiling-to-floor oil painting of the Hindu god Shri Nathji. The consul was very cordial. He asked me about my education in the States and life in general. My answers must have pleased him as he then handed us the visa papers along with a large brown envelope contain-ing Milan's x-rays. He instructed us to carry the x-rays with us because US immigration would need it at our port of entry. We were on our way to our land of destiny!

CHAPTER 11
A New Journey

It was about time to get back to reality. The newlyweds had to settle down, and I needed to start earning a living—in the United States. We began our trip to the US on November 7, 1968, leaving from Bombay for New York via Athens, Copenhagen, and London. Both of our families, relatives, and friends were at the Bombay airport. Rita, the travel agent, had put together an ingenious travel itinerary. We were guests of the airline for overnight layovers in Athens and Copenhagen. Athens was our first stop. After settling down in a hotel room, we took the Athens by Night bus tour. The next morning, after visits to the Acropolis and the original Olympic Games sites, we returned to the hotel, rested for a while, and took a plane to Copenhagen. As instructed by the US Consul in Bombay, I was carrying Milan's x-rays in my hand. During the flights it stayed in the overhead luggage compartment, and while getting down in Copenhagen, I forgot to pick it up. When I realized my mistake, it was too late. I spent the entire evening and night trying to track down the envelope. My phone bill was staggering. The good news was that the envelope was handed over to us when we caught our next flight, from Copenhagen to London.

It was very cold in Copenhagen. Before taking the city tour, we rushed to a ladies' clothing store to buy a coat for Milan. The least expensive coat was for $350 and I had no choice but to buy it even though the cost was equal to a two months' rent for a one bedroom apartment in New Jersey. After the purchase of the coat and paying the phone bill, I was almost broke. The city tour included a visit to the statue of the mermaid. I took Milan's picture in her sari and new winter coat at the statue. It sits in our bedroom as a memento of a very happy memory. A new version of Milan's photo at the same site has been added from our trip to Copenhagen in August 2008, almost forty years later. In London we stayed with Milan's favorite aunt, Madhufoi. We enjoyed two days of sightseeing. Milan had the opportunity to experience what the life of an Indian family was like in a foreign country. She finally got to eat some good Indian vegetarian food. The flight from London to New York City was uneventful, and going through immigration and customs was easier than I expected. My friend Lalit was waiting for us at the terminal. Lalit had completed his BS in chemical engineering and was working in New Jersey. His apartment was in Jersey City. We had a flight to catch to Boston within a couple of hours. My friend Gulab, now a full-fledged doctor, and his wife, Anu, now lived in Boston. I felt Milan would be more comfortable in Boston if she had Anu for company while I looked for a job. Reality really had set in. I started roaming the streets of Boston the morning after we arrived. I would kiss Milan as I left the house. Gulab's two-year-old son, Parag, a fast learner, started kissing a neighborhood girl whenever she arrived to play with him!

Bharat & Milan

There were not that many food companies in Boston, and many of the personnel agencies I visited directed me to New York. Finally, I left for New York City. Milan had gotten very comfortable with Anu, and I felt at ease leaving her behind. After landing at the New York airport, I barely made it to the Roth Young personnel agency before closing time. Roth Young specialized in the biological science field. I talked to the only agent who was still in the office and pleaded for help. I told him to ignore my doctorate degree on my résumé. I was desperate and would take any job, even at the bottom rung of the ladder. It was about five minutes before five. He called a few people he knew but could not get anyone. The last call he made was to Al Knipper, manager of product development at Nabisco Research Center in Fairlawn, New Jersey. Al picked up the phone. He was told of my background and of the urgency for me to get a job, along with my willingness to start as a technician. I was asked to see Al at 10:00 a.m. the next morning.

The next day, before going to work, Lalit dropped me off at the Nabisco Research Center. Al Knipper was a very courteous, congenial person. I felt I could be honest with him about my sense of urgency, as a newly married man, to get a job as soon as possible—any job. Within half an hour, I had a technician's job in Al's lab. I accompanied him to see the head of the research center for the final formalities and to discuss my salary and benefits package. As I entered the director's office, I saw the name plate on the wall: Dr. Norman Desrosier, the author of a book I was very familiar with, *Principles of Food Preservation*. Al introduced me, presented a synopsis of my résumé, and expressed his desire to hire me. Dr. Desrosier gave an approving nod and asked Al to go over the salary package. I thanked him, and before leaving, I asked him if he was the author of *Principles of Food Preservation*. He practically jumped for joy and asked me how I knew. I mentioned that I had attended CFTRI, Mysore, and that we used the book as our main textbook. CFTRI is a world-renowned institute. Dr. Desrosier was extremely happy to hear of his book being so highly recognized outside of the United States. I could still see the sparkle in his eyes as he asked Al and me to sit down. Then he asked more questions about my background and the academic work I had conducted so far. He asked Al to take me around the research center and to have me meet all the department heads and to see who wanted me the most.

The Nabisco Research Center had five major departments, with a total of 250 scientists and technicians. I spent the next two hours discussing my background with each of the department heads. Unknown to me, I had five job offers, all within one building. Finally, Dr. Ronald Morch and Dr. Ralph Sand of the Basic Research Department convinced Dr. Desrosier that I fit their needs the most. The Basic Research Department wanted to start a flavor chemistry division to study flavors of Nabisco products, especially Ritz crackers. I was given my salary package: $9,800 per year, with two weeks of vacation after a year. I accepted it gladly, with only one question: When do I start? They told me I could start anytime I wanted to. I told Dr. Desrosier that I had just arrived from India, and all my books and belongings were in Logan, Utah. Also, my wife was new in the United States, and I desired to have her see the country and meet my American friends before settling down with work. He said that I could start anytime I wanted to and that I should bring my airline tickets and hotel receipts for reimbursement, and he would take care of it. I was happy beyond belief. I could not believe that four hours could change my fortunes so drastically. I knew I had a job at Nabisco. Recognizing Dr. Desrosier as the textbook author had helped open a door of opportunity. I did not worry about the salary, what bothered me the most was the two weeks of vacation at the end of the year. I couldn't see keeping Milan home for an entire year without a vacation. So I, a broke man but one with a new job at hand, decided to have the vacation first; the job and money would have to wait!

After calling Milan with the good news, I spent the rest of the afternoon with Dr. Sand and Dr. Morch. My assignment as the head of a one-member flavor chemistry department was to analyze the flavor components of Ritz crackers and compare them with the competition, Keebler and Townhouse crackers. Then, and to this day, Ritz crackers' flavor components, the ones that the olfactory sensors in the mouth pick up, are the most pleasing compared to the other crackers on the market. The research project I was assigned was to identify those flavor components of Ritz crackers that created the superior sensation. There was no intention of changing or artificially flavoring the dough; it was just basic research, and I was excited to undertake the project.

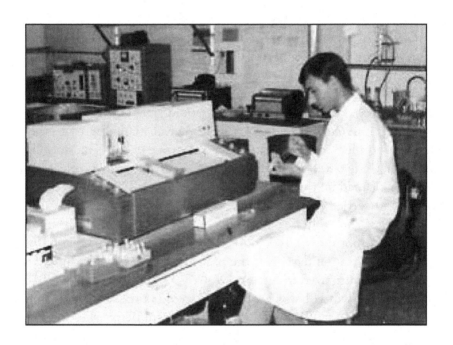

Bharat - Research Chemist

Milan arrived in New York that evening, and we stayed with Lalit for a day. We left for Chicago to spend a couple of days with Bill and Linda Nabors. Bill had been my classmate at Utah State. The next stop was Logan, Utah. After arriving there I called Bill Wayman at Pioneer National Bank. I also called Dr. Salunkhe and Ted Kindred in Hyrum. Bill Wayman was excited to hear my voice and was particularly happy when he heard I was married and was in Logan with my wife. He asked us both to come to the bank right away. We went to his office, and I introduced Milan to him and chatted about my time in India. Then he asked me to join him to the president's office. As we entered, Bill announced, "I told you my son would be back. Here he is—Dr. Shah, a research chemist with Nabisco." Understandably, the president had been doubtful about my actually returning to the United States and had questioned Bill's wisdom in cosigning a $5,000 note on my behalf. I made the president happy when I told him I would start paying back the loan by January 1, 1969. Bill invited us to dinner at his home that evening. After a good meal and a pleasant visit, we drove to the Kindreds' house that night. Ted, Betty, and their kids were very anxious to meet Milan. They had cleaned up their eldest daughter Rebecca's bedroom for us and Milan and I settled in at their home.

The next morning as Ted and I were going through my diary of wedding and honeymoon days over the past five months, Betty came up behind me and murmured in my ear, "You're going to be a father!" I could not believe the words I was hearing. We were taking all the precautions, planning to start a family once I got settled down. Betty asked me to look toward the backyard, and I saw Milan bending over near a bush, throwing up. That day in Hyrum, Utah, was the beginning of a new chapter in my life!

We headed toward the campus in the afternoon to see Dr. Salunkhe and Dr. Olson. I showed my lab to Milan, and she met most of my former colleagues. Dr. Salunkhe invited us for dinner at his house that evening, where we met Mrs. Salunkhe and their children. Meanwhile, Ted and Betty Kindred had gotten a list of my friends and professors from my roommates, Najam and Arun. Two days later, on a Saturday evening, the

Kindreds threw a reception on our behalf. It was a great gesture. Milan was feeling good and quite satisfied with the company I kept and the love she received from my friends and the families we had visited. To some extent, my goal of her experiencing the American way of life was being fulfilled. Milan still did not have her last and most important question answered: Where was my house and my personal belongings? The closest thing I had to a house was my old car, still parked in the Kindreds' garage. I finally showed her my car and opened the trunk, telling her that its contents were all I had: some clothes, books, a tape recorder, some tapes, and a transistor radio. I told her I did not have a house. As I spoke, I dared not look into her eyes lest I see any possible disappointment or unhappiness, and I just walked away. Milan accepted my statement as presented without any criticism or negative comment. She just kept quiet and we walked back in the house.

By that Sunday evening, we were back in Jersey City at Lalit's apartment. On Monday morning, after two weeks of vacation, I reported to work at Nabisco. Every evening when I returned to the apartment, I saw Milan looking lost. I asked her if she was all right, and she asked me how long we would be staying in that apartment, which was dark and didn't even have a window. To get to the street, she had to walk down a dark corridor. She didn't dare, so she spent every day in that dark place all alone. I asked Lalit if there was anyone we could move in with until I found something close to my work. Lalit suggested that I call Amrut Lala. I had met him in Athens, Ohio, when I visited Lalit. Amrut had been married for a year or so and had a little son. The family lived in Metuchen, a town in South Jersey. I called Amrut and explained my circumstances to him. Apparently, Amrut and his wife, Sumati, had lived in Lalit's apartment themselves when they had arrived as newlyweds from India. Amrut insisted we move in with them immediately. Grateful and without hesitation, we packed our bags, and Lalit drove us there. When we knocked at Amrut's apartment door, his wife, Sumati, opened the door. She saw Milan and said, "Oh, Milan, is that you?" The girls had met in India; Sumati lived in the same town as Milan's best friend and college roommate, Manju. During one summer vacation, the girls had spent time together. This situation made me feel much better. The Lalas gave us their bedroom, and they slept on the floor in the living room. We shared groceries for about two weeks. I bought a used Pontiac and commuted to Fairlawn from Metuchen. Meanwhile, I kept looking for an apartment close to my work so that I could come to see Milan during a lunch break. We rented a furnished attic apartment in Glenrock, just a five-minute drive to my work.

Milan and I finally had our own place. Our routine was established: morning tea and then lunch together, as the Nabisco Research Center was so close. After lunch, Milan would make some Indian dishes and would sit at the one and only window, waiting for me to return home. We would have dinner and then go for an evening walk. After the first three or four days of our new life, I saw dishes were piling up in the sink. I made an indirect comment that the dishes needed to be washed, but to no avail. Finally, a couple of days thereafter, when I came home for lunch, all the plates and silverware, furnished to us by the landlord, were in the sink. Milan asked me in frustration, "When will my *bai* (cleaning lady) arrive?" I quietly replied, "I'm your only *bai*, and I'm your only *bhai* (home servant)." Here was a princess who had never even lifted a plate after a meal, and now she was in the richest country in the world without any housemen. By the time I returned home from work that evening, the dishes were done!

There was an apartment complex, the Tivoli Garden Apartments, in Parsippany, where at least ten Indian couples lived. Moving there would make my commute to work at least an hour long, one way. However, I wanted Milan to have some friends, and soon we moved to Parsippany. There we made a few friends. Pradip and Mira Shah became very close friends of ours. We had no furniture and were sleeping on the floor on a mattress borrowed from somebody. There was a Two Guys store in Clifton on Route 46, a straight shot from Parsippany. One evening Milan and I went there. We wanted everything to set up the apartment, but I had no credit. I showed my Nabisco pay stub, and credit was granted instantly. The next day the apartment was beautifully furnished. Every month thereafter, I sat with my checkbook and a slew of coupon books to make our monthly payments, including a payment to Pioneer

National Bank. However, since Milan's pregnancy had started before I joined Nabisco, the pediatrician fees and upcoming hospitalization expenses weren't covered by insurance. As far as home shopping and her personal needs, I was very careful not to let Milan know how tight my budget was running.

One morning, skipping the chain of command, I went straight to Dr. Desrosier's office. I asked his secretary if I could see him. He liked me so much that he actually rushed to the door to receive me. In a few words, I told him of my financial difficulties. My salary was adjusted to $13,500. The only thing he asked of me was to keep up the good work. That evening the dinner at home was special. I had a $3,700 raise, more than 30 percent in one shot! Milan and I were very happy. I saw my budget getting a little easier to live with.

Milan was doing very well in our new apartment. We had found a good pediatrician in Parsippany who was very fair with his charges. Our friend Pradip's mother, who was visiting from India, had a soft spot for Milan. When Pradip and Mira were at work during daytime, Milan took care of the mother at our apartment. She threw a baby shower for Milan at Pradip and Mira's apartment. On August 10, 1969, a Sunday morning, Pradip and I were planning to go shirt shopping, because Arrow shirts were on sale. Milan heard our phone conversation. She was in a bed resting and pleaded with me not to go shopping. I called the doctor's office. Milan was about two weeks from her delivery date. The doctor told us not to worry. I was about to leave and Milan pleaded, crying, saying it seemed like she was passing water. I called the doctor again, and he told us to rush to the hospital immediately. I had already practiced all possible routes to the Morristown Hospital from our apartment in case of a delay because of road construction or emergency work. I could drive to the hospital blindfolded. Once at the hospital, Milan was immediately taken to a labor room. I was allowed to go with her. Sonogram technology had not arrived by 1969, so we didn't know the sex of the upcoming child. Both of our families had a history of having a girl as the first child. Milan and I imagined our first child would be a girl, too. As I sat in the labor room, holding Milan's hand, a nurse asked us what name we had chosen for the child.

I answered, "Mona."

The nurse said, "But that's a girl's name. What if it's a boy?"

And suddenly we were in an unexpected quandary. Without any further thought, we decided to come up with a name, combining both of our names. We took "Mi" from Milan and "t" from Bharat. Mit means love, and when you end it with "esh," it means the best: Mitesh. Within twenty minutes of entering the labor room, Mitesh was born, one week before our first anniversary. I still dread the thought of going shirt shopping!

New Parents

My priority at the end of the day, after leaving Nabisco, was to rush home and play with Mitesh. It was August 18, 1969, our first anniversary. I had completely forgotten the significance of the day! While driving home from work that evening, I realized that I had missed Milan's birthday, which was a day earlier, August 17th, and that I was just about to miss our first anniversary, too. I immediately pulled my car into Woodbridge Shopping Center. There was a jewelry shop just as I entered the door. I asked a saleslady to show me a diamond ring. She asked me for a budget. I said one hundred dollars. That was still high for my budget, but I thought I could wing it. She took me to a counter and showed me some rings. I liked a ring with a one-carat diamond in a unique setting. That was it. I got it wrapped, and as soon as I reached home, I proudly presented it to Milan. She loved it. A few months later, the diamond started turning gray. I took it back to the jewelry shop and complained of the diamond's quality. The girl told me that for one hundred dollars, all I get would be a 'Diamonair' not a real diamond. I felt ignorant and didn't ask her to explain the difference. I didn't ask for a refund, either; I just brought the ring back home.

Mitesh was a happy baby. He loved food. While we fed him baby food with a spoon, he would scream, complaining about the time it took to scoop another spoonful from the jar. We took him all around with his playpen, even for weekend poker games at friends' houses. Milan was a good poker player, and she enjoyed such outings. One day, it dawned on me that I had promised Milan we would return to India after a year in the States. I reminded her of the promise and mentioned that it was time to pack up our bags and leave. I remember vividly that at that moment she was feeding Mitesh his favorite baby food. She replied without hesitation that she wasn't leaving; she loved our life in the United States. I told her in that case, she needed to write a letter to my father and tell him just that. My father loved getting his first letter from his daughter-in-law. He was happy to know that she was quite content with life in USA and said it would be alright if we wanted to settle here. He also wrote that as much as I had talked positively about life in the United States, and now knowing Milan felt the same way, one day they would plan to visit us.

CHAPTER 12
All Is Not Well!

I was making good progress at Nabisco. The Ritz cracker flavor components project was moving on track. I was being recognized as one of the bright scientists at the lab, and my colleagues regarded me with respect. I was chosen to provide the butter flavor for the famous Nabisco butter cookies. The product development lab tested many of the flavors I provided and finally chose one to use for the pilot test, using a minimum of one ton of dough to run a production test. I used to bring grocery bags full of hot butter cookies home and give them out to all in the neighborhood. I was known as the "butter cookie man."

On a brisk fall day in October of 1970, I received a letter at work from my father. It said that Milan's dad had passed away as a result of a massive heart attack. He was only forty-six years old and I was completely devastated. I loved him so dearly, more so than anyone else, including my parents. I found a private corner where I cried my heart out. This was a man who loved me so much—ever since I was a young boy, he had taken me around as though I were his own son. This was the man who had taken the brunt of his family's criticism when he permitted Milan to marry me. This was the man who trusted me when I said in my letter that I would take care of his daughter. This was the man I had most desired to bring to the United States and proudly show him around, just as he had always done for me. I wanted him to see firsthand how happy Milan and I were and thank him for being a major supporter of our union. Even today, I think of him frequently, and I still feel sad about that unfulfilled desire. Although I had no money in my bank account to pay for their tickets, it was my decision to send Milan home to see the family. I borrowed the money from Lalit.

Within two weeks, Milan and Mitesh left for India to visit her widowed mother and young siblings.

My progress at Nabisco continued. The company headquarters in Manhattan had come up with a program for interaction among managers from various divisions: research, production, marketing, sales, accounting, and so on. The meetings were held in Manhattan every Tuesday for three months. I was Dr. Desrosier's favorite manager and was chosen to represent the research center. Every Tuesday I would be in Manhattan at the Nabisco headquarters. Heads of various divisions would make presentations to explain the workings of their divisions and their interrelation with the other groups. I was learning a lot, meeting quite a few other managers, and enjoying my career growth.

One Tuesday, Dr. Gian Jamb, director of marketing, came to speak to us. I figured he was either from India or Pakistan. He saw me in the group, and after the speech, he invited me for lunch. As we talked it became clear that both of us were from India. As I gave him a rundown of my life so far, I added that I eventually wanted to start my own business. Working for someone for the rest of my career was not in my blood! He proposed that I join him and two other partners and start a gift store. I liked the idea, and for the next few Tuesdays we worked out a deal for me to join the gift store business. One evening I met the other partners, Gary Swartz, an attorney, and Steve Nehlig, an airline pilot. All of them lived in East Brunswick, New Jersey. We decided to open a store at the Shopper's Mall on Route 18 in East Brunswick. One Tuesday, Gian suggested that if he could get me moved to the Marketing Department, it would be easy for us to work together on our business. I liked the idea even better. The following Tuesday, Gian and I went to Human Relations and had a meeting with the director. Gian talked about a need for a technical person in his department; I mentioned that I liked marketing more than research. I told him that the marketing work was more exciting than the research work. Thereafter we waited for the approval of my transfer. The gift store was given a name: Faraway Places Imports, Ltd.

Greed overcomes all senses. Every Friday over the last three months, I had seen pink slips flying at the research center. Many of my friends, including my boss, Ralph, had been laid off. The word was that business was slow, and each division was asked to cut the payroll. I was too naïve to understand until, one Friday in February, I received a pink slip. I was told it was because I had more interest in marketing than in research, and unfortunately, the marketing department was also laying off personnel. They couldn't fulfill my request for a transfer. I tried to see Dr. Desrosier, but he had left for the day. Maybe he did not want to see my face. I understood his disappointment in me after all he had done for a young immigrant from India. That thought in itself pained me. My behavior was unacceptable, and I regretted it. A beautiful career path came to a sudden stop. I was devastated. The following Monday, I was back at the Roth Young Personnel Agency for them to help me find a job. Nothing was coming through. After a few days, I went to Yash Paul Sohi, my friend from Logan, who had opened up an Indian restaurant on Twenty-Eighth and Lexington in Manhattan. I explained my frustrations and told him of my desire to return to India for good. Milan and Mitesh were already there. He was the person who was responsible in convincing me to stay in the United States and to look for another job. He asked me to stay with him and his wife, Dorothy, and encouraged me that things would work out fine.

During the middle of March 1971, Milan and Mitesh returned from India. Milan had lost weight. Mitesh was speaking Gujarati and singing Hindi songs. They had been gone almost six months. Mit didn't remember who I was. On the night of their return, I played with him all night long, as it was his daytime in India. He finally became convinced that this man had something to do with his mother! The next morning I got dressed and left the apartment as if I was going to work at Nabisco. I was actually leaving to look for a job. I got home in the evening after knocking on quite a few doors. The routine continued for a week. One evening when I returned, Milan asked me how my job was going. Without hesitation I told her how wonderful my work at Nabisco was and that I had expectations of another raise soon. She then handed me a letter from our friend Pradip, who was out of the country on a job assignment. Someone had spilled the beans about me being jobless, and he had sent a letter of consolation. I looked at Milan and told her the whole story as tears fell from my eyes. She made me a cup of tea and calmed me down. I told her about our partnership in the gift store, and she actually liked the idea of having our own business.

A week before Milan's return, I had been interviewed by Gordon Carlson, director of quality assurance at RJR Foods. RJ Reynolds Tobacco Company out of Winston-Salem, North Carolina, had decided to diversify into other businesses besides tobacco. They had acquired Hawaiian Punch, the Chun King brand of Chinese food, Patio Mexican food, and other food companies to form a subsidiary, RJR Foods. The company headquarters were in Manhattan, and the quality assurance lab was in Hoboken, New Jersey.

On Monday, a week after Milan's arrival, I was called by Lynn Sant, Gordon's secretary. She asked me to come to the lab that afternoon to meet her boss. Once there, she guided me into Gordon's office with her fingers crossed. Within ten minutes I was offered a job as manager of quality assurance. There were many applicants for the job. Gordon told me that it was Lynn who had recommended me because, according to her, I was very cordial and well-mannered. I thanked her for getting me back on my feet. I had a family to feed! Gordon asked me to meet him the next day at the Newark airport to join him on a trip to Winston-Salem. There we met our colleagues at the Reynolds building and at the Whitaker Park Research Center. Gordon explained to me that in a year or so, RJR Foods personnel would be moved from Manhattan and Hoboken to Winston-Salem.

In April of 1971, we moved to East Brunswick to be near our other partners at Faraway Places. We built the store ourselves, working at night. Gian left for India and Thailand on a buying spree. I had asked my father if he could arrange for some money to be given to Gian as partial payment toward my partnership. He met Gian in Bombay and gave him 25,000 rupees. I did not know how he raised the sum. We opened the store in June 1971. I had no more money to put toward the partnership. As part of a deal, Milan and I were paying by working twelve hours a day each Saturday and Sunday. An Indian couple lived above our apartment. They had no children. Sunanda, the wife, loved Mitesh and was happy to keep him every weekend when we were at the store. All the partners and their wives were taking turns in managing the store during the weekdays. Weekends were ours to manage. Milan and I did not know what a weekend was for almost a year. Milan was by far the best salesperson of us all. I commuted to Hoboken from East Brunswick, driving an hour and a half each way; it was still worth it. My job was going well. I had a personal secretary, a food preparation helper, a chemist, and a microbiologist. As the head of the QA lab, my job was to make sure the manufactured product met the standards of quality before being released to the market. I enjoyed the work and the frequent visits to the plants with Gordon.

Sometime in June 1972, Gary and Steve, my partners at Faraway Places, asked me to meet them at Gary's office. They explained their discontent with Gian because they could not get along with him. They asked me if I would remain with them if we offered to buy Gian out. I had the same issues with Gian and was willing to go along with them if they came up with the money and I could pay them back later. We agreed to invite Gian for discussion. During our meeting, Gary did the talking and made an offer. Gian accepted it with the condition that he was to be paid off in two weeks. Gary and Steve agreed. During those two weeks, the ladies at Gary's and Steve's houses changed the guys' hearts. Their main concern was that Gian knew the gift business, and none of us knew it that well. At our next meeting with Gian, Gary explained our reasons not to go forward with our offer. Instead, he asked Gian if he would buy us all out. Gian agreed with a condition. Monthly payments to each of us would be spread over a period of three years, without any interest. We had to agree. All the labor of the whole year, not knowing what the weekends were, and the money my father had put in on my behalf evaporated within minutes. But for some reason, I was relieved. I did not want Milan and myself to work in a discontented environment and in a business without a vision for growth.

In August of 1971, I received a letter from Navapur. My brother Sanjay was diagnosed with having Hodgkin's disease, a cancer of lymph nodes, and his body was full of tumors. Sanjay, an ardent devotee of Shri Rang Avdhut, was a seventeen year-old freshman at Wilson College, and had been rushed from Bombay to Navapur after experiencing severe stomach pain. I immediately left for India and met my father and Saryu's husband, Chandrakant. We visited almost all the oncologists in Bombay to discuss the treatment options. Chemotherapy was the only treatment option in those times. Pappa asked each doctor of Sanjay's chance of survival and status of his daily life during the treatment period. Their honest answers convinced us that there was not much hope of his survival and his pain would be significant during chemotherapy. Pappa made the decision not to let Sanjay suffer anymore and let the nature take its own course. Sanjay was provided care at home in Navapur. His condition deteriorated slowly. I visited my family every couple of months. Saryu and Chandrakant were the pillars of support for my parents during the time of unprecedented emotional toll. During his last days in August 1972, Sanjay had gone into a coma. One evening he woke up, looked around the room and motioned my mother to come and sit on his bed. Sanjay rested his head on her lap, looked at Bapji's photo hanging on a wall, paid respect with hands clasped and took his last breath. I found solace in my belief that my baby brother was a divine soul who had chosen to take birth as Manubhai and Induben's son. The loss of my only brother and the youngest child in our family was very painful for me, and most especially, for my parents.

CHAPTER 13

RJR Foods, Inc., Winston-Salem, North Carolina

The timing for a move away from Faraway Places could not have been better. Within weeks the announcement came from the RJR Foods headquarters that all of us would be moved to Winston-Salem, North Carolina. Soon after, Gordon and I left for Winston-Salem to make arrangements for a location for my lab and to interview candidates for lab technician positions. We spent two days there and completed our work. I met a few of my colleagues from the tobacco division who would be moving to the foods subsidiary. Bob Appleyard was one who offered to help with my move. The parent company, R. J. Reynolds Industries, was a top-notch company. Everything related to the move was very professionally done. Milan, Mitesh, and I arrived in town and spent five days for orientation and for familiarization with Winston-Salem. In many ways it was a company-paid vacation, and we really needed it.

A month or so later, on August 7, 1972, we arrived in Winston-Salem by car. We had bought a brand-new 1971 Plymouth Duster for $2,500, no AC, no radio. Those luxuries cost $300 more, which we did not have. I had asked Bob Appleyard to find us a place with a stove and refrigerator. We needed to warm milk for Mitesh, who was three years old, and be able to cook in case we got tired of eating out. He chose the Winkler Motor Inn at 600 Peters Creek Parkway. We were assigned Room 501 for a rent of seventy dollars per week. It had a stove and a refrigerator and was a perfect setup for our purposes, with a grocery store and a Laundromat across the street and a lot of restaurants nearby. We stayed at the Winkler for three weeks; then we moved to the Village Apartments and rented a brand-new two-bedroom townhouse. All the young couples with children were in one section, where the backyards were back to back and the area was fenced. The backyard area was the playground for the children. Mitesh made new friends, and he was enjoying life in the new city. I, on the other hand, found the town to be too quiet and boring. I was missing Manhattan; even though we didn't live there, it was there whenever we needed to feel the hustle and bustle of city life. For the next six months, I sent my résumés to companies in large cities—New York, Chicago, Miami, and Los Angeles. The companies that wanted to hire me couldn't match the manager's salary I received at Reynolds even if they offered me a director's position. I got the message: Reynolds's salary and benefit package was one of the best in the country. I decided to stay put and make Winston-Salem our new home.

It was a good place to raise a family; there was a sense of welcome in the town. One day, while driving to work, I was tailgating cars and changing lanes, even though the traffic was nothing compared to New Jersey. I was pulled over by a traffic cop. When he saw my driver's license and tag were from New Jersey, he asked me if I was a part of the RJR Foods group that had moved from New Jersey.

I said yes.

He said, "Sir, welcome to Winston-Salem. This is a small town without any traffic, and you don't need to speed here. Have a good day, sir." After having lived in New Jersey, I could hardly believe the kindness and sincerity of the policeman.

The RJR Christmas party in 1972 was held at Bermuda Run Country Club. I, being a manager-level employee, received an invitation. This was the first time in my life I got to visit a country club, so I was excited. I got my suit pressed and to make sure I would reach the entrance gate on time, I scoped the area twice by car. When I finally reached the gate in the evening, a security guard asked me if I was there for the Reynolds party. I said yes. He gave me a military salute and welcomed me. I was pleasantly surprised and taken aback a little bit. Here was a white officer giving a salute to a brown man. I remembered the London front desk clerk who "didn't have a room" for me. I remembered the restaurant just outside of the UT Knoxville campus with a sign declaring, "Dogs and Coloreds Not Allowed." Winston-Salem was definitely a breath of fresh air. I parked my car and went inside the ballroom. All the top brass of RJR was there. One couldn't tell, looking at the suits, who was a manager and who was the chairman of the board. As I made my rounds, I felt very welcome. At one point I did meet the chairman himself, who told me, "Thank you for coming." I loved this company, and I loved this town!

RJR Foods Colleagues

Soon after the Christmas party, Milan, Mitesh, and I left for India for a two-week vacation, my first visit home since my marriage. My parents were happy to see me and my family. I sat down with my father to tell him all about my job, my title, and my salary. After that, anybody who came to see us was bombarded by his proud bragging about his son who was now a big officer in America and making so many rupees a year. US dollars, converted into rupees, sounded like such a large number that the local crowd in Navapur couldn't fathom it. My father went on and on, and my sisters, overhearing him from the kitchen, scolded me for telling him too many details. I finally had to tell him not to repeat the big numbers too loudly. Frankly, I was financially stable but still only making a modest salary.

The Sagbara episode had still not ended. Pappa had won the case in the high court after twelve years of struggle. The government of Gujarat had appealed the verdict at the Supreme Court. The monetary situation had not changed. The money cabinet still had a box with only a few rupees in it, and all the other shelves were empty. For my father I had brought a sense of pride by being financially secure in a foreign land. This was a moment for him to be happy after a very long period of hardship.

After visiting Milan's family in Kadod and making a pilgrimage to Nareshvar and Goddess Ambaji's temple, we returned to Bombay for our flight to New York. During the flight Milan and I noticed Mitesh's body had swollen up, and his eyes were bulging out. We were worried sick but there was nothing we could do until we reached Winston-Salem. Once we arrived, the pediatrician diagnosed Mitesh with having Nephrotic Syndrome. The polluted water in India had affected his kidneys. As treatment, he was put on a heavy dose of the harsh drug, prednisone. Milan and I checked his urine daily for the level of protein he was losing. As he lost protein, he would retain water and his body would swell up. As he took the medications, he would lose water and swelling would go down. Mitesh went through three different sizes of clothing. Milan and I blamed ourselves for not taking good enough care of Mitesh in India. We hated to see his suffering; at times we even feared we would lose him. Mitesh was in the excellent care of Dr. William Lorenz at the Baptist Hospital in Winston-Salem. He was the one who kept us constantly informed of Mitesh's progress and convinced us that he would eventually recover. The disease ultimately lasted over twenty years and basically ruined Mit's childhood. We never took him back to India.

Sometime around March 1973, Mitesh started telling his friends he was going to have a brother. The neighborhood ladies started asking Milan if that was true. Milan had no sign of pregnancy but, the pregnancy was confirmed a month later, with the delivery expected in October. Milan's mother, Ushaba, arrived in August; it was her first trip to the United States. Milan's brother Pankaj was married to a girl named Bharti. Natvarbhai, her father, was also visiting the United States to see his other daughter in Chicago. We invited Natvarbhai to Winston-Salem. All of us, with pregnant Milan, went to Disney World. Natvarbhai and I became good friends, even though we had a significant age difference. Ushaba felt very much at home, as I personally treated her like my mother. Little brother Rajesh was born on October 20, 1973. The name Rajesh was chosen by Mitesh, as he had seen many Indian movies during his trip to India where his favorite actor was the famous Rajesh Khanna.

My work at RJR Foods was going well; I had received a couple of raises. Reynolds had a program whereby a maximum 10 percent of one's salary could be automatically withdrawn from the payroll check, and Reynolds would contribute 30 percent of the withdrawn amount and buy Reynolds stocks on one's behalf. I had participated in this benefit program from my first day of employment. Reynolds stocks went through a period of unbelievable growth. I could walk in anytime to the Reynolds Credit Union and borrow 95 percent against the stock's value in my account, at a much lower interest rate than the general market. One day in December 1973, I happened to be at the credit union. My account had a good enough balance for us to pay 10 percent down for a new home. With two children in the family, Milan and I decided to look for a house. Our first house in America was at 3018 Loch Drive, Winston-Salem, North Carolina. It was a four-bedroom brick ranch house with a basement in the beautiful neighborhood of Town and Country. The price tag was $49,900 with $5,000 down. The first piece of furniture was a Ping-Pong table, for which Milan has not forgiven me yet. Next was a basketball hoop. Later came all the other furniture for the house. We priced the drapes for the entire house, and the estimate was $12,000! Milan took lessons for drapery making at Forsyth Technical Institute. She bought the material for $200; I bought a used Singer machine for $100. Labor being free, the total cost of the entire house drapery was $500, with rods and other accessories. We hung the drapes ourselves. Forsyth Tech was my hangout on the weekends. I took all kinds of classes there. I was the best mechanic for small engine repairs, and my teacher, Brock, loved me. He would mess up the rhythm of a carburetor and ask every student in turn to come and fix it. I would be called last. Within seconds I would have the engine running the smoothest of anyone in the class.

During one of our trips to India, I had insisted that my parents come and visit us. They arrived in the summer of 1976 at our home in Winston Salem. When they saw our well furnished four bedrooms home, they were very happy. They knew well that this would not have been possible if I had stayed in India. My father's first question was whether we had applied for US citizenship or not? I told him that Milan and I had naturalized immigration status and the papers to apply for citizenship were ready, awaiting his approval. That, for sure, meant that we had no plans to return to India and wished to permanently settle in US. Without batting an eye, he firmly announced that we should apply immediately and this place was our destiny! Milan and I were so happy for his blessings and proceeded to apply for US citizenship. My parents stayed with us for three months. During their stay we took them to all the tourists' attractions from New York to California, Florida as well as Canada. Pappa and I went to my office at RJR Foods and I had him meet with all my colleagues. He was very impressed with the way I was being liked and respected at my place of work. They returned back to India as happy and contended parents.

I was making good contacts with various department heads at Reynolds. Don Harris, director of purchasing, became a good friend and invited me to join his weekend poker club, made up of Reynolds directors and vice presidents. We played seven-card stud poker where only five cards are used to play and make bets. One night I was betting for a "high" as well as a "low." Everyone at the table thought the Indian was going to lose his shirt. After a few rounds of bets and raises, when I opened my cards, their jaws dropped open. I had a real high and a low! That was followed by momentous cursing. They didn't know I had played poker from the age of twelve on the streets of Kadod. Through my expert card playing, my reputation at RJR went up a notch. A few members of the group also played tennis. I joined the team and played with my boss's boss, Dr. Dave Maggison, VP of research and development.

A couple of years after we moved to Winston-Salem, my boss, Gordon Carlson, retired. Richard Morgan, who was a manager in the tobacco group, became director of QA and my new boss. Richard and I got along very well. He was also a member of the poker group. When RJR bought McDonald Tobacco Co. in Canada, besides tobacco operations, some food processing plants were also acquired. Those plants were in Montreal, Toronto, and Windsor. Following the acquisition, I received a promotion to become an area QA manager for Canadian plants, besides being a head of the QA laboratory in Winston-Salem. I would visit Canadian plants every three months. As I represented the headquarters, my reception in Canada was exceptional. The plant managers loved me, as my approach to quality control was simple: If whatever infractions I found were corrected on the spot, that wouldn't go into my written report. If I found something that needed time to correct, I would report it as a joint decision. I received full cooperation from all plant managers. Hank Dosegar was a plant manager at a Chun King plant in Windsor, Ontario. During one visit Hank told me that a quality control manager had resigned, and technicians were running the department. I asked Hank to write a request to Richard Morgan for help with a new hire.

Meanwhile, I had received a call from Natvarbhai from India. He mentioned that his son-in-law Rohit, who lived in Chicago, had a degree in microbiology. He could not get a professional job, however, because he had a degree from India; he was working on a line in some manufacturing plant. When Hank asked Richard for help in hiring a QC manager, Richard asked me if I could find someone. I said I would look into it. I contacted Rohit and learned of his background. I asked him a few questions on microbiology, and it seemed he knew his stuff; however, he had never worked in a food company.

Throughout my life I have kept in touch with most of my friends, especially those with whom I got along well. I had helped Gulab Patel and his friends Thakor and Ashvin a lot with their studies at UT Knoxville when they had arrived from India. Gulab lived with a large group of Gujarati students, and I was their grocery man. I knew Gulab was in Chicago working for Libby McNeill & Libby, a food processing company. I called Gulab for help. He replied, "Anything for you, Bhidu!" I asked him to contact

Rohit, pick up some Chun King products, and teach Rohit the methods of quality control. After a few weeks of coaching, Rohit was ready. I prepared Rohit's résumé, highlighting his experience in the food industry in India and other required parameters to be a quality control manager. I gave the résumé to Richard, who forwarded it to Hank; and within a week, Rohit and his wife, Devyani, moved to Windsor. After a month or so, I went to Windsor for a plant inspection. I was in Hank's office, and Rohit was asked to come down. I was meeting the man for the first time in my life. Hank was very happy with Rohit. When Hank was on the phone, I asked Rohit in Gujarati how it was going, and he said excellent. I was happy to be a matchmaker, even though my methods of making the match were questionable. Rohit started as a manager of quality control. A few years later he became the plant manager. A couple years after that, Reynolds sold that plant to a Hong Kong company. That company ran into financial trouble and decided to sell the plant. Rohit became the new owner of the plant in 1991. Today the plant is the headquarters of a family business to inspect food products on behalf of the US Department of Agriculture and Canadian Food Inspection Agency before passing the largest commercial border between Windsor, Ontario, and Detroit, Michigan. Rohit is now retired, and his two sons, who were babies when I visited Windsor, are running the family business. Even after thirty years, if someone asks when and how they got into this unusual business, Rohit and Devyani will name Bharatbhai and repeat the tale with joy in their hearts!

CHAPTER 14
Business Ventures

Since arriving in Winston-Salem, my desire to have a business of my own had grown stronger and stronger. The only country I really knew well was India. I thought of the possibility of importing certain items from there to the United States. My father was involved in a new business—a papaya plantation. He had a contract with a farmers' co-operative to grow papaya trees. Every morning, raw milk was collected from the skin of green fruits and stored in refrigerated containers. Pappa supplied the milk to a processing plant for drying and refining. The refined product is called papain, which is a digestive enzyme used for meat tenderization. It is also used as a clarification agent for beer, to give it a crystal-clear appearance. The United States is the largest user of papain. My father put me in touch with the management at the processing plant. I formed Quality Foods International with an office at home. The papain price is set according to the enzyme activity of the finished product. I set up a lab in my garage, and as time permitted, I contacted various meat processors, brewing companies, and brokers who did brokerage business with the users of papain.

One of the administrators at the papain plant in India contacted me to help him develop an export business in the United States and asked for me to be his agent. I took time off from RJR when he arrived in Winston-Salem, and we visited many of my contacts in Chicago and Milwaukee. For the entire year, I worked as a middleman, spending my own money to travel to various places, and kept the man in India informed. Then, all of a sudden, everything got quiet. There was no reply from the buyers or the supplier. I soon found out that the administrator in India made direct contacts with the US buyers I had represented and left me out of the deal.

RJR Foods used large quantities of mung bean to produce bean sprouts for Chun King products. It also used large quantities of shrimp for egg rolls and shrimp chow mein. As the head of the QA lab, I was in charge of checking the quality of those raw materials before they were used in production. I knew the quality parameters as well as the price of those raw materials. India is one of the largest producers of shrimp and mung bean, and I made many trips to India to develop contacts with the suppliers. The US Food and Drug Administration (FDA) had put restrictions on shrimp imports from India because of microbial contamination. The government of India would not allow export of food grains, even if the supplier would grow mung bean for export purposes only. My father and I made special trips to Delhi to try to convince the Ministry of Agriculture, but to no avail. After spending two years of vacations and travel money that wiped out all of my savings, Quality Foods International was closed for business for ever.

Our neighborhood on Loch Drive was a friendly one. Every once in a while three or four families would get together for a weekend cookout. Max and Phyllis Smith lived across the street from us. Max was a large man with a gregarious spirit and a southern charm. He was an owner of Mother and Daughter stores in North and South Carolina. The company sold ladies' footwear. Max had read somewhere that India was a major supplier of leather goods. One day he asked me if I could get him leather shoes from India. Max gave me a couple of sandals as samples, as they were very popular in the United States. I took those samples to India to show them to manufacturers and get pricing on them. After visiting Milan's and my families in Kadod and Navapur, I went to Bombay to contact shoe manufacturers. A family friend, Janak Shah, was in the leather goods export business. Janak and I met some shoe manufacturers in the area and found the reception promising. Before leaving for New York, we agreed for Janak's company to select a production facility and to conduct quality control during production. For this work, I would pay Janak a 3 percent commission. I left the sandals with him so he could have samples made to ship to Winston-Salem. Two pairs of samples arrived by air within a month. One pair was size five, and the other was size eight. However, the problem was that the size five shoes were larger than the size eight shoes. Furthermore, I had a hard time contacting Janak. I would call Janak's office at midnight our time, which would be 10:30 a.m. Bombay time. I would hear from a secretary that Janak had not come in yet. I would call at 2:00 a.m., 12:30 p.m. their time, and would be informed that Janak had gone for lunch. I would make calls all night long and might catch him once in two to three days of trying. Phone lines were terrible during the seventies; one had to practically shout through the roof for the other party to hear. Janak's advice was that on my next trip, I should bring the "lasts"— shoe forms in plastic or wood—so he could manufacture the correct size shoes for the US market.

Other than the size problem, the finish of the shoes was good. I showed the samples to Max, and he liked them. My cost was eight dollars per pair, delivered in the United States, duty paid. Max suggested we form a company as partners. He would buy the shoes at sixteen dollars per pair for his stores. He could sell them for eighty dollars per pair, at a 500 percent profit. Hence, even during a half-price sale, he would make a 250 percent profit. He would also help me get contracts with other shoe distributors. The business had great potential. I named the company Feel Me—"feel" for Phyllis, Max's wife, and "me" for Milan. In March 1976, Max and I headed for India. Max had a contact at a shoe factory in Ohio. We got two sets of lasts, one set for narrow widths and the other for regular. When we reached the Bombay airport, the customs officer stopped us for carrying lasts with us. I had documents with me showing that Indian manufacturers had asked us to bring the sizes so that the shoes could be sized for the US market. The officer still wanted to set their value and charge 200 percent duty. I argued that we were here to help Indian exports, and the country needed the foreign exchange. He confiscated the boxes and asked us to return the next day at ten in the morning and appear at customs court to argue our case in front of a judge. Max was totally puzzled by the unreasonable attitude of the customs officer. This was his first trip outside of the United States. I had hoped to find some link to the customs office so we could get the boxes with a little bit of bribe money. I could not get anybody to help me. We appeared in front of the judge the next morning. I showed him the requests for the lasts and explained that we were helping Indian exports. The judge declared: No duty, 3,000-rupee penalty. Max jumped out of his seat and argued that this was ridiculous—and it was. If there is no duty, what was the penalty for? Max thought that it was $3,000. In seconds I converted the rupees into dollars, and it came to about $250. I asked Max to sit down and calm down. We paid the penalty and picked up the boxes. Later I explained the exchange rate to Max and told him that we could handle it. The lasts were very important to get the business going. We spent a couple of days in Bombay with Janak and visited a few manufacturers. Max was impressed by the response of the suppliers; they were young men, fluent in English, and understood the strict quality control process for exporting to the United States.

Our next stop was Agra. This city, where the Taj Mahal is located, was a major center for leather goods production. We spent the night at the Holiday Inn Taj, and in the morning we went down to the lobby to meet a couple of manufacturers. We all went to the hotel restaurant for breakfast. Max and I ordered scrambled eggs, toast, and coffee. The other two gentlemen were vegetarian and ordered accordingly. All those days in Bombay, staying with a Hindu family, Max had only vegetarian meals—and very unfamiliar dishes at that. He finished the eggs in about two bites and asked me how many eggs had been on his plate. I said may be two or three. He signaled the waiter to come to our table and asked him to prepare fifty eggs, scrambled.

The waiter did not understand the number, so he asked me in Hindi, "Sir, did the white sir ask for fifteen or fifty?"

I replied in Hindi, "Fifty."

Thereafter the conversation continued in Hindi.

He said, "But…sir?"

I said, "Yes, fifty."

Then he asked, "Is the order for all of you to share or only for him?"

I replied, "Only for him."

He rushed back to the kitchen, and during the next ten minutes, everybody from the kitchen, including the head chef, came to take a look at Max. Later on the general manager came to ask if we were getting proper service; in reality he had come to see the fifty-eggs man, Max.

Max and I returned to Winston-Salem to await the arrival of the sample sandals from India. Once the samples arrived, I became a salesperson on the road, meeting the distributors Max had lined up. Meanwhile my work at RJR was still going fine. I oversaw a department of about eight people, and everybody's duties were spelled out in detail. I would take a couple of days off to go and try selling some shoes. I found out that the competition was tough, but even worse, I realized I wasn't that good of a salesperson. The other problem was money. I needed cash to get a letter of credit from a bank; only then would a supplier ship the goods from India. Max had no money, either. He was my so-called partner, but he didn't even have the money to buy airline tickets. I footed all the bills, hoping one day the business would make money. It had to! A pair of shoes that cost eight dollars would sell for sixteen, and right there was 100 percent profit. I just needed one order to recover all the expenses.

Meanwhile, Janak sent me some samples of very fine-looking shoes from Bombay. The manufacturer was Kanodia Enterprises. The owner, Vijay Kanodia, was planning to visit the United States to develop more export businesses and intended to visit us. Vijay arrived in Winston-Salem and stayed with us for a couple of days. He and I struck a very friendly chord. He was a rich man by either Indian or US standards. I was a chemist, trying to create long term financial security for my family. I was open and honest in showing my desire to get my own business started and had found shoes from India a viable undertaking, except I had no money to get a letter of credit for a large order. Vijay had developed trust in me and offered to ship the goods without prepayment. At last I saw the light at the end of the tunnel. Three months later, I was in Bombay. Vijay and I reached Kanpur, another leather goods center in northern India. The factory shell was ready, awaiting machinery from Italy. I was satisfied that there was good potential for future business with Vijay.

I would make these quick trips to India by leaving on Thursday night from Greensboro, North Carolina, and returning back by Tuesday evening. In about two years' time, I had been to India at least six times, spending nights sitting by the phone and being back at RJR at eight in the morning. All my vacations and our savings were devoted to developing a viable shoe import business. The upside was that Milan had about a hundred pairs of shoes, all in different styles, as the samples came in her size. Max knew I was putting all my time and effort into getting good-quality shoes from India. Buying them at sixteen dollars a pair, he knew he would make more money than I would by supplying him. Around April of 1977, he placed an order for five thousand pairs of one style of sandals. I sent the samples to Janak. Vijay's factory was still not ready. Janak placed the order with one of the suppliers we had visited together. I knew the administrators, and they were trustworthy, quality manufacturers. The letter of credit to be drawn was for $40,000. I saw the opportunity to double the money in three months. I went to Wachovia Bank and took out a second mortgage on the house, then went on to RJR Credit Union and borrowed against my stocks. I added a little money from savings, and I came up with $40,000. The letter of credit was sent to the supplier's bank in Bombay.

Within a couple of months, my order was ready to be shipped. Janak had supervised the production, and the product quality was good. I received a letter to that effect. The shipment was placed on a cargo ship leaving for Wilmington, North Carolina. As soon as the shipping documents were submitted to the bank in Bombay, $40,000 was withdrawn from Wachovia. Somehow I had thought of getting insurance for the cargo at sea. I had never done an import business, and as I think of it today, I have no idea how I came to the decision that led me to insure the $40,000 of cargo, representing all of my savings, that got placed on that ship. .

One day, in the middle of August 1977, I happened to be at home during lunch. The phone rang, and I answered. The heavy-voiced gentleman asked if this was Feel Me.

I did not understand the question. I said, "What?"

The voice got angry. "Is this Feel Me?" the man repeated.

All of a sudden I realized that the call must be for the shipment from India. I said, "Yes, yes, this is Feel Me."

The man grew even angrier and said, "Take these goddamned boxes out of here!"

I said very calmly, "Sir, what is wrong?"

He said, "They are all mildewed and stinking like hell."

He turned out to be a customs officer at Wilmington port.

I asked him for his phone number and told him that I would be in touch. The next thing I did was call the insurance company. The gentleman I talked to asked me to wait for him to figure out what was required for the shoe shipment from India. The next day I got a call from him. He asked me if all the pairs were in plastic bags. I said yes. Then he asked if the bags had silica gel tablets. This is where all the years of learning chemistry got distilled in two seconds. I knew that silica gel is a dehumidifying agent. The bags should have had the tablets but I had no way of verifying if they did or not. I responded that, "I believe they should sir, every bag should have had silica gel."

He said, "That answers all my questions. And for forty thousand, I am not traveling to Wilmington to look at the shipment. Where do I send the check?"

What a relief! I had realized the shoes were made in the monsoon season, when the manufacturer had nothing else to do. I was a small buyer, anyway. That experience broke my back. Any attempt to do business with India ended in frustration and disbelief. I was persistent, up until now, in trying at all costs to get into my own business. All that was needed at this time was to make one more trip to India and insist that production of my shoes would not be done during monsoon season. I could have been doubling my money at every shipment.

This was a moment for soul-searching. I realized I had neglected my family life for many years. The Shah family had no vacations for almost ten years. We did not even go out to eat. Every time Milan came to pick me up at the Greensboro airport, she looked tired. The aura she had reflected before had gone dim. The boys, sitting in the backseat, looked meek and gloomy and had no desire to say hello to daddy or give hugs when we reached home. Where did the blessing come from that told me to get the cargo insurance? The day I received the check, I prayed a lot to god for saving me and my family. I folded Quality Foods, Feel Me, and everything in between. Thereafter, I just wanted quiet time with my family, going to movies, picnics at Tanglewood Park, to the theater and Music at Sunset at Reynolda Gardens. RJR provided the stability and money to do all that. I was a happy family man, and I realized that is all I needed in life!

CHAPTER 15
RAAM Corporation: A New Beginning

Milan and Manju Bhoola were roommates from 1964 to 1966 when they were at the University of Baroda. Manju was the one who had pushed Milan to reply to my first veiled love letter. Manju's brother Mohan, who lived with his family in Johannesburg, South Africa, visited the girls during a trip to India. Because of the loving sisterly relationship between Manju and Milan, Mohan also considered Milan his sister. In March of 1977, Mohan and his friend Nanu were in the States to check on a motel property in California that Mohan had made an investment in. Apparently, the property was doing well. Milan invited him and Nanu to come visit us in Winston-Salem. Mohan said that if she would line up a hotel property for them to look at for investment purposes, he would love to come. We talked to the broker who had helped us buy our house. She was confident she could find a property investment for our friends. Mohan and Nanu arrived in Winston Salem where I met Mohan for the first time.

I would leave for RJR in the morning and be back at 5p.m. Meanwhile Mohan had a file on me—what I did, how much I made. Milan had given him the numbers. As soon as I arrived home, my small home bar would open, serving Johnny Walker Black Label on the rocks. Our guests would start talking about how wonderful the hotel business was and put pressure on me to get into that business. I hadn't forgotten my nightmare where I stayed at an Indian-owned dump in San Francisco, and my answer at midnight each evening, when these discussions would finally end, was always, "No thanks!" When Milan and I went to our bedroom each night, I quarreled with her and asked her to tell her "brother" to lay off; I wasn't interested in the motel business. The routine continued for the four or five days Mohan and Nanu stayed with us.

The night before leaving Winston-Salem, Mohan realized I wasn't at all interested in buying a motel. But Mohan didn't take "no" for an answer, and his "sister," Milan didn't, either. Mohan worked on convincing me that I should become a real estate agent dealing only in commercial properties. His reasoning: Indians who had settled in African countries like South Africa, Kenya, Uganda, Zambia, and such were slowly moving out. Those who arrived in the United States would look for motel properties. And the precedent had been set by some Indians with the surname Patel, who had invested in motels and done well. Mohan's final point: with my knowledge of Gujarati and English, I would make a good broker, making money on the side in addition to my salary at RJR. I wouldn't have to quit my job. For the first time in five days, I agreed with his plans, and that made him happy. I actually liked the plan and started gathering information on how to get a broker's license in North Carolina. I took real estate lessons at night for the next six months, and after passing the state licensing exam, I received my broker's license.

The Travel Host motel on Highway 52 in Winston-Salem was close to my office at RJR. One day, in November 1978, at lunchtime, I met the owner, Mr. Ron Oakley, and inquired if his place was for sale. He sounded positive. I contacted a family visiting from Zambia and looking for a motel investment. For one reason or another, I could not make fast enough progress for Mr. Oakley—he had to close the deal before December 31—and a Chinese family from New York bought the Travel Host. I met with Mr. Oakley during the first week of January 1979 and asked him to help me locate another motel property in town. He knew Jim Myers, owner of the Winkler Motor Inn, on Peters Creek Parkway. Winkler was where Mitesh, Milan, and I had stayed for three weeks when we moved from New Jersey in August of 1972. He called Mr. Myers on my behalf and convinced him I was a good man and a straight shooter, unlike many other brokers. I met briefly with Mr. Myers that evening at his home. As I was working at Reynolds and was interested in making a little money on the side, Jim Myers agreed to give me a listing for six months. The next day I acquired an official form and got it signed, a process I had failed to follow in my dealings with Mr. Oakley. The ninety-unit property was priced at $1,250,000, with a $125,000 down payment.

So now I was a broker with a legitimate listing—even if it was only for six months and not exclusive. Through family connections in India, I was introduced to Chhaganbhai Patel, who had a motel in San Francisco. I asked him if he would be interested in a motel in Winston-Salem. He was very interested and asked me to get him the last five years of its financial data. I got the figures from Jim Myers and sent a copy to Chhaganbhai. During the next few months, I received lowball offers of around $650,000 and, later, $750,000 at the most from Chhaganbhai. Afraid that I might get kicked out of his house, I did not present the offers to Jim Myers. Meanwhile, I tried other contacts throughout the country. At that point, the Indians in the hotel business had dealt only in smaller properties, and a million-dollar investment was not part of the mind-set. There really wasn't a legitimate offer I could take to Jim, and after a very quick six months, the listing ended. Every time I tried to meet Jim Myers thereafter, he was rude, abrupt, and had no desire to meet me anymore. I stopped calling him and decided being a successful salesman was not one of my roles in life. I did not enjoy pleading with potential buyers or sellers. Milan kept on pushing me to call Jim, and I became angry every time she did. I just didn't want to deal with those types of insulting situations anymore.

One Sunday afternoon in June of 1979, Milan quietly asked me to call Jim. I looked at her and hesitantly called Myers's home. Jim answered the phone, and I asked him to allow me to come to his house and explain what kind of offers I had received. I told him that I hadn't brought them to him for fear of insulting him. He asked me to come over. We sat down in his living room. He asked me about my job at Reynolds. I explained my work, and he seemed to be impressed. I showed him a couple of offers, and he was not interested in those numbers.

Seemingly out of thin air, he threw a question at me, asking what country I was from. I said I was from India.

"Are you a Hindu or a Muslim?" he asked.

I said, "Sir, I am a Hindu."

121

"Are you one of those guys who believe in reincarnation?"

"Yes, Hindus believe in reincarnation."

"Does that mean that you keep coming back over and over? When does the damn thing end?"

I said calmly, "Mr. Myers, I really don't know where I was in my previous life and where I'm going to be in my next. There is a saying, 'What you sow is what you reap.' I believe the Hindus have taken the philosophy of Karma—fruits of one's deeds—seriously. It means that if one doesn't pay for the bad deeds in this life, that person will certainly return to pay for it in his next life."

Jim Myers just jumped. "Bart, that's exactly what the Bible says: 'So thou sow, so thou reap.' How wonderful that is. So what is the name of your scripture, like our Bible?"

"That is the Geeta, sir."

From there the discussion went on, with Jim bringing up a theory in the Bible and asking me if Geeta reflected the same principles. I was not (and still am not) a serious student of Geeta, but I professed to be very well-versed and always found a parallel philosophy to put forward. He loved the conversation. I found out later that he was a born-again Christian and was attending a Bible school. For the next two months, every Sunday at about two in the afternoon, I would get a phone call: "Bart, Betty has made some apple pie, and I know you like it. Why don't you come over, and we'll have pie a la mode and some coffee." I would go see him, hoping he would renew the listing with me. Instead, we would run through Hindu and Christian philosophies and find parallels. I remained very careful not to point out any conflicts between the two religions' belief structures.

Finally, on July 25, 1979, when I finally felt comfortable talking about business again, I handed him a contract to sign and renew the listing with me. He replied, "Winkler is not for anybody else, Bart. You buy it. It's for you, and I know you will make money." I was totally taken aback by the statement. There was an excitement in the air; my blood started moving fast. I had studied five years of data and realized the price Jim Myers was asking was reasonable. I replied, "Mr. Myers, I'd buy Winkler for the price you are asking, but I do not have the one hundred twenty-five thousand dollars' down payment that you need."

He countered, "Well, how much do you have?"

I said, "About forty thousand dollars"—the same amount that I had raised for my venture on shoes from India. It was the same source of money: a second mortgage on the house, Reynolds stocks, and whatever cash we had on hand. He said that I may have to come up with a little more. In the meantime he was going to find out from his accountant whether any taxes would be due that year upon sale of the property.

Milan had visited India in December 1978. I had asked her to, if she could, visit Nareshvar, Rang Avdhut's ashram. I had not asked her to do any special prayers for us. On her own, she did fifty-two prayers of Dattabavni at Nareshvar. It was Bapji's recommendation and Nareshvar tradition to recite Dattabavni fifty-two times, to represent fifty-two weeks of a year, to get fruitful result in any undertaking. As I left Myers's house, for some reason, I started praying and reciting Dattabavni, asking for help in this endeavor and to not fail. Then I remembered Milan's visit to Nareshvar and thought maybe she carried the blessings as a result of her prayers. I thought of how the sequence of events had changed things at the beginning of January 1979, after Milan had arrived back from India. I went home and told Milan about my discussions with Jim Myers. She was excited and was ready to go forward with the deal and to help me raise the money for a down payment.

The first phone call was to Mohanbhai in Johannesburg. He committed $10,000. I contacted Gulab and other friends. Meanwhile, Jim Myers had drafted a two-page contract, all in his own handwriting, ready for us to sign. He went through the details with me as he read through the contract. Jim was going to finance the deal, which made it much easier for me. I wouldn't have qualified for a loan that size anyway. Jim had addressed an issue of nonpayment of mortgage installments. In case of a foreclosure, he would only take the property back and would not touch my personal home or belongings. This was a condition he had put in himself, without me asking for the waiver. I was amazed by his generosity. I didn't need to read the document any further. We both signed it and drove to the office of his attorney, Sam Booth. Jim told him of our agreement, gave him the two-page contract, and asked him to make a legal document based only on the written pages. Sam said he could not represent both of us. Any party could sue him in the future if not satisfied with the outcome. Jim and I both gave him assurance in writing that we will not.

I started analyzing the numbers that Jim Myers had given. I pulled out numbers on the Sheraton that I had when Mohanbhai visited Winston-Salem and had looked at investing in that hotel. Milan and I started our own investigation. Sheraton and Winkler were on I-40, one exit from each other. Milan and I would wake up at one in the morning, pick up the kids from their beds, and put them in the backseat. We would drive to the Sheraton and count the cars and then go to Winkler and do the same. We would be back home by 2:30 a.m., put the kids back to bed, and go to sleep ourselves. The next day I would analyze the occupancy based on number of cars in the parking lots and compare the numbers with the data on hand. We would repeat the process at least three times a week and continued for several weeks. This was our process to conduct a feasibility study.

During all this period, I had not inspected Winkler to see what the rooms looked like, so I asked Jim to show me some rooms. He did not want the employees to know that the Winkler may be sold. He asked me to meet him in room 408 at 8:00 p.m. I knocked at the door of room 408, and Jim opened the door. This was a suite with a round ornamental bed with a mirror at the headboard, mirror on the ceiling, a red Jacuzzi tub on the side, and a bar in another corner. The walls had red wallpaper with gold decorations. I had never seen a hotel room like that. Jim sat on a large sofa chair and asked me to sit on a chair opposite him. As soon as I sat down, the chair broke. I picked up the broken parts and stacked them against the wall. At least now I knew the condition of the furniture. There was no need to look at any more rooms. I was just too anxious to make a deal knowing that there would be some cost and hardship. Jim and I stepped outside and went toward the pool fence. As I looked at the area, Jim asked me, "How many children do you have?"

I said, "I have two sons. Mit is ten, and Raj is six."

Then he asked, "Is it all right if we transfer the car to your son when he gets to be sixteen?"

"Mr. Myers, the car...what car?" I asked.

He laughed. "Oh, I probably haven't told you that yet."

The Winkler and the Dodge dealership next door had once been one property, Parkway Hotel and Parkway Chalet Restaurant. During hard times, the previous owner had sold the restaurant to Chrysler Corporation for a Dodge dealership. Jim had bought the hotel. There was only one entrance from Peters Creek Parkway to enter the two different businesses. A dispute had arisen over the ownership of the entrance. The land survey showed that the entrance was on the hotel side of the property. A settlement was made for the use of the entrance by the dealership, whereby the Dodge dealership gave the hotel owner one car for his use, to be exchanged for a new car at the time of the arrival of new models every year. Jim asked me if his daughter Tina, who was a front desk clerk at Winkler, could continue using the car until Mitesh turned sixteen. I wasn't looking for a new car; I wanted the hotel. I said I would have no problem with that. Next he asked me if Tina could continue working for us. I said by all means, as long as she wanted to work.

Then we got down to more significant business issues. Jim asked, "How much money have you come up with?"

I said, "Around seventy-five thousand dollars."

He asked, "Could you raise an additional twenty-five thousand?"

Apparently, the attorney had advised him that I needed a larger down payment.

I replied, "I would not be able to raise that much more; I have exhausted all my resources."

He responded as though I had not spoken, announcing, "We will close on Thursday, August seventh. Bring two checks with you."

What a coincidence! Exactly seven years earlier, on August 7, 1972, baby Mitesh, Milan, and I had arrived from New Jersey and had settled at Winkler Motor Inn, ready to go to work for Reynolds.

Milan and I formed a new entity to acquire Winkler, RAAM Corporation. RA was derived from Rang Avdhut, and AM represented goddess Amba. We needed all the blessings we could get to help us with this venture!

Milan and I were on our way that morning for the closing. I was so excited that I did not know how fast I was driving on Reynolda Road. The traffic cop got me at the bottom of the hill, and I got a ticket—my first in Winston-Salem.

We finally reached Sam Booth's office. There we met Jim and Betty Myers. I gave two checks to Jim, a cashier's check for $75,000 and a personal check for $25,000. Sam entered $100,000 as a down payment on the closing statement. We all signed the documents and left for Winkler. There, for the first time, I met Tina, General Manager Mary Pence, and other staff members. Jim handed over all the master keys for the property. Then he pulled out the $25,000 check from his wallet, put it in my shirt pocket, and said, "Pay it when you can." I had no words to express my gratitude. Milan and I had become hoteliers. We were happy and excited about our new enterprise. However, at that point, I was in more debt than I ever could have imagined. In addition to what I owed Jim and Betty Myers, I owed friends about $40,000 and all of my personal assets were invested into the motel as well. Still I was at ease and was ready to celebrate the occasion. After school was out for the day, we picked up Mitesh and Rajesh and brought them to Winkler. We conducted a family prayer and then cut a cake; the inscription on the top read, "God Be with Us!"

The next morning I was back at work at RJR. I had not mentioned the Winkler deal to anyone at work, our Indian friends, or our neighbors on Loch Drive. It remained a secret to all until the deed records at Forsyth County showed a change of ownership at Winkler. A reporter with the *Winston-Salem Journal*, a local newspaper, came looking for me at the hotel. The desk clerk must have said that I would be at the property around six in the evening. That was my routine. Eight to five at RJR, go home, have a cup of tea and some snacks, and arrive at the hotel around six. I would stay at Winkler till about ten, then go home, have dinner, and go to bed. The next morning I would be back at Reynolds.

Winkler - Myers & Shah Family

Milan would drop the kids at school and then be at the hotel till about two in the afternoon. Then she would pick up the kids and go home. Milan had never worked in India or in the United States. She remained a homemaker, especially so she could spend time taking care of our children herself. She did, however, come from a business family. She knew what to look for and how to ask pertinent questions whenever there was any doubt. She would leave me notes about her observations, written in Gujarati, on my desk. Once I was at the hotel, I would look into the matters that she had questions on. One time a front desk clerk signed a delivery receipt for one thousand pounds of laundry detergent. Milan could not find the shipment anywhere on the property. Meanwhile, I was watching the accounts receivables going up and up, and it seemed like no one was paying the bills. I had asked Mary Pence many times to try to collect the amounts due, but she came up with various excuses. The maintenance crew was drinking on the job, and customer complaints were not being handled in a timely fashion. Nonetheless, business was strong. We were running 90 percent occupancy, and even Sundays were busy. We generated net cash flow through the months of August to October that almost matched my annual salary of $30,000 at RJR. Milan and I were very happy. We saw ways we could tighten up our operation of the hotel and began making changes to our business. First Mary Pence was let go, then the maintenance crew and a few unenthusiastic housekeeping and desk staff members, and we began a search for replacements.

One Monday morning in October 1979, I was entering the RJR product development center where my office was located. Betty, a lobby receptionist, announced, "Ah, here comes the real estate tycoon!"

Bharat -1979

I said, "Betty, what are you talking about?"

"Oh, don't tell me you have not seen the newspaper," she shouted, and pulled the paper out. There was a big picture of me, standing under the Winkler sign on the front page. The headline read: "Reynolds Chemist Buys the Old Winkler." I remembered the *Journal* reporter who had gotten hold of me one evening at the hotel. He had asked me a few questions and taken that photo. I was nervous when I got to my office. My secretary, Debbie, informed me that Chuck wanted to see me. The central lab had been moved under Dr. Chuck Pheil, director of R&D. When I knocked at Chuck's office door, he looked up and asked me to come in and close the door. I sat down across from him at his desk. He looked angry and said, "I thought you were a goddamn research chemist."

I said, "I am, Chuck, and despite what you read in the newspaper, I haven't allowed my work to be affected."

He said, "I know that, and I have no problem with you making a real estate investment in town. But, damn it, why Winkler? Did you do any research on the property you now claim to own?"

I asked what he meant by that question. Chuck recited the entire past history of Winkler Motor Inn. During the late sixties, the hotel bar, the Gold Club, was a prostitutes' hangout. Madge Roberts was a madam with a client list that included some top names in the Southeast. The VIP clients would be whisked from the Reynolds airport on a helicopter that landed on the rooftop of the back building at Winkler. The VIP client would then be entertained in Room 408. The same red and gold ornamental room with mirrors all over, where I met Jim Myers for the first time! Madge Roberts and her cohorts were arrested during the winter of 1969, three years before the Shah family arrived in Winston-Salem. When Chuck stopped talking, my heart stopped too. I was devastated and could not talk any further. I told Chuck I had no idea what I was going to do next and left his office. I went back to my office and closed my office door. Though I felt complete remorse, I really had no choice but to continue running the place; I had put my life's savings plus a substantial debt into it.

I regained some composure, remembering when we lived there, in Room 501, for three weeks in 1972. No one had come knocking at the door with a proposition and a dangling purse in hand. As many times as we were there in the wee hours of the morning, counting the number of cars parked, we hardly saw anybody up and around. Even as we were negotiating on buying the property, the old bar was being used as a storage room. Besides, I was at the hotel until 10:00 p.m. every night—and sometimes until 1:00 a.m., if I wanted to talk to our night auditor, Jim Swicegood, a hardworking, loyal employee. Walking the property at those hours, I had never seen anything like what Chuck described.

It had to be in the past, and I told myself that I should not be worried about that part of Winkler's history. The challenge at hand was to improve the operations and maintain the high occupancy level. When I got home that evening, I did not tell Milan about my discussions with Chuck Pheil. Instead, I showed her my picture and read the front page story of the Real Estate Tycoon!

CHAPTER 16
Learning the Ropes

When Mary Pence was fired, she threatened she would take business away with her, moving it to her next job. And it seemed she made good on her threat. By mid-November 1979, Winkler occupancy was down so much that the place felt deserted. I was very uncomfortable. There was not much work at the property, and I could not concentrate on my work at RJR. Nights became sleepless, as I spent the time going through different scenarios of "what ifs."

One night, around two in the morning, I felt Milan was tossing and turning.

"Are you awake?" I asked.

She said, "Yes."

"Why, Milan? Are you thinking something?"

She replied, "Not really; nothing important."

"Are you thinking about the property?" I asked.

"Yes."

"Are you worried about the business at the hotel and paying the mortgage?"

In a subdued voice, she said, "Yes."

I asked her to get up and listen to what I planned to do.

Both of us sat in bed with the covers over our feet. I explained to her that if we could not make the mortgage payments, and Myers fore-closed on us, I was prepared to lose Winkler as well as the $40,000 of our own money we had used toward the down payment. The house had enough equity that if we sold it, we would have enough money to pay back the friends from whom we had borrowed and that will be the right thing to do. That would mean that the family would have to move back into an apartment. With profound apologies, I told Milan of my utmost regret that after finally giving her, Mitesh, and Rajesh a house to live in, I could not maintain our lifestyle. My job at Reynolds was intact, and there would not be a problem feeding the family. Without any hesita-tion or questions, Milan replied that she had no problem moving back to an apartment. The boys were young, and by the time they grew up, we would have enough saved to buy a house again—maybe a smaller one. Milan's response was unexpected. I was ready for a hard, drawn-out argument at two in the morning about what I had done to the family. Instead, she provided moral support at the right time. I believe that has been the strength of our marriage and has been proven many times. I was relieved. I told her that if the scenario was agreeable to her, then I was not worried at all. I told her to pull the covers back over us and we should go to sleep.

Greensboro, North Carolina, less than 30 minutes to the east of Winston Salem, had a large number of motels owned by Patel families from India. We knew them all. During the latter part of November 1979, we had a Diwali get-together in Greensboro. I was making rounds to shake hands with everybody, and I intended to talk business with a couple of friends who had been in the motel business for some time. Individually, I talked to Babubhai Patel, Sitaram Dakoria, and Dhansuk Panwala. I asked them how business was. Each replied that with this being winter, there would not be much activity until March of the next year. All of them were leaving for India for a couple of months, to return to the United States in March 1980. They had saved enough money during the first ten months of the year to pay for their mortgages during the winter months. A desk clerk would run the property, and if there was enough revenue to pay for utilities, they would be paid; if not, they would catch up upon their return. At that moment I realized I had no real understanding of the business cycle in the hospitality business. I thought we were supposed to run 90 percent occupancy year round. I felt relieved. On the way home that night, I happily told Milan what I had learned. I told her that we were paying the mortgage as well as the utility bills in spite of lower occupancy. The only difference was that we did not generate as much cash flow as we did during the summer months.

Milan had made an observation that whenever a weekly tenant left a room at Winkler, we would rent out the same room on a daily basis. The daily rental provided double revenue per room per day compared to the weekly rate. We began to reduce the number of weekly rentals a few at a time, started renting them at the daily rate, and saw our revenue go up. Milan also figured that if we raised the daily room rate by only one dollar, we would make as much additional revenue in a year as my yearly salary at Reynolds. I had continued working at RJR as a safety net in case of a disaster in the new venture, like I had gone through in the past. My new understanding of the hotel business cycle and my worst-case scenario strategy gave me enough strength to take the next and most important step in my life. I would be saying good-bye to my career as a food scientist, and the years in school reaching to a doctorate level would be left behind. On the Monday after Thanksgiving in 1979, I went to see Chuck Pheil. I explained that I urgently needed to become a full-time manager at Winkler because my own money and my friends' money were at risk. As he listened to my lengthy overture, he pulled out a folder from the left drawer. He told me that he had been watching my performance after the newspaper article. He was very impressed that I had maintained a superior work performance level even after taking on the arduous task of running a motel. Chuck told me that I was due for a raise. I thanked him but instead asked to be relieved of my duties; I was resigning. He asked me to hire a replacement and to train the person before leaving. He also told me to feel free to run to the motel to take care of any urgent business. At the next food technology convention in Philadelphia, I hired Cliff Coles, a microbiologist from General Foods, to take over as head of the central lab. Cliff was an accomplished, knowledgeable microbiologist and was a people person. We worked well together.

Three months later, on Friday, February 20, 1980, I was given a formal send-off by RJR Foods's research and QA department. Sometime during the summer of 1979, Reynolds had bought Del Monte Foods Co., a company with a sales volume of $1 billion, headquartered in Walnut Creek, California. RJR Foods, with a sales volume of $250 million, was a baby compared to Del Monte's volume and reputation. Monday morning after my departure on Friday, an announcement came that drastically changed the careers of all of RJR Foods personnel. All of them would be moved to California to join the respective groups of Del Monte. There would be no salary adjustments except moving expenses. On the other hand, Del Monte personnel's salaries were raised to match RJR Foods salary structure. The cost of living was at least 20 percent higher in Walnut Creek compared to Winston-Salem. That meant everyone who decided to move to California took a 20 percent salary cut. I only heard the news and then was told of some rumblings of disgruntled employees through Cliff. My life at Winkler had gotten so busy that I really did not have any interest in knowing what was happening with the colleagues I left behind. I often think about Friday, February 20th being my last day and Monday, February 23rd, being the day of bad omen for many at RJR Foods. What a saving grace.

By January 1980, I had made substantial changes to the team and performance at the Winkler. The second shift, covering 3–11p.m., was the most important shift at Winkler. Now I needed someone presentable and with a fresh outlook on hospitality service, so I put an ad in the *Winston-Salem Journal*. Meanwhile, I started managing the second shift myself. The very day after I placed an ad in the newspaper, a young woman named Carol Conrad came to Winkler. I was checking in a group of construction workers, and Carol stood at the end of the line. I looked at her and acknowledged her presence by waving my hand at her. I thought the Winkler clientele was changing, and I was happy about it. When her turn came, she told me, "I've been watching you taking care of your customers. You can go home now; I can do your job." I was taken aback by her comment. She wished to apply for the desk clerk position. I asked her to fill out the application form and told her that I needed some references, too. Carol was a master's student in philosophy at Wake Forest and was working on a thesis toward getting her degree. As she turned in the application, she told me that I didn't need to talk to anybody for a reference except her father, who was a school principal in upstate New York.

When I got home that night, I called the number Carol had given me. As he picked up the phone at the other end, the gentleman said, "Just go ahead and hire her. There is no better person that that."

I burst out laughing and said, "Sir, I am Bart Shah."

He said, "I know." Mr. Conrad was a very funny man. Besides being a high school principal, he was a certified gemologist. We talked for a while, and after I hung up, I called Carol and asked her to report to work the next day. She needed only a couple of hours of training before I was able to go home. Thereafter there was no second shift for me. Carol's presence at the Winkler made a great impact in changing the customer mix. We started getting senior citizens, salespeople, and families to stay at Winkler. Service went up, room rates increased, and thus - so did our revenue and profits.

I was free to become the businessman I had wanted to be my whole life. The first thing I did was to join the Winston-Salem Chamber of Commerce and the Convention and Visitors Bureau. The mayor of Winston-Salem would brief the chamber members every Thursday morning on things happening in the city, especially new business projects, who was coming to town, and how many employees they would hire. As it happened, I was the first one to know in the hospitality industry of the potential business coming into town. I would contact those companies and would get their commitment for business. Knowing the level of service we had at Winkler, I had asked for only second- or third-tier employees to stay with us. My business card read, "Bart Shah, General Manager." The bottom of the card read, "Come, Stay with Us!"—the welcome phrase I had coined—in large letters.

I got to know many of the business executives in Winston-Salem. Martha Wood, then the mayor of Winston-Salem, had come to know me through the Chamber and knew of changes we had made at Winkler. I had the opportunity to meet a superintendent of Norfolk and Western Railway at one evening reception at the Chamber. N&W ran a railroad track between Norfolk, Virginia, and Winston-Salem, hauling coal and other commercial goods. The superintendent asked me about my business and then listened to my story about how I got into the motel business. He loved the fact that an immigrant family had ventured into a business totally foreign to their education and were serving as an example of American entrepreneurship. He asked me if he could visit Winkler the next morning. Milan and I greeted him when he arrived. We had Indian masala tea, coffee, and snacks prepared for him. Upon his request, we showed him the property. At the end of the two-hour visit, we were told to work out a contract with the local station manager for the N&W crew to stay at Winkler. Within two weeks we had the crew staying with us. The revenue from N&W was about $12,000 per month. That actually paid our mortgage to Myers. The arrangement lasted for almost twelve years. The superintendent retired during the latter part of our contract, and as a new property had opened near the station, it was awarded the contract.

At the beginning of 1980, RJR Tobacco Company made an announcement that the company would spend $1 billion during the next ten years to renovate all the cigarette manufacturing plants in Winston-Salem. That meant that the city would see $100 million of spending per year for ten years to come. It was a big boost to the economy for a town with a population of 140,000 at the time. When I resigned from my job, I had no idea that my future would still remain tied to RJR Industries. We were filling the rooms at Winkler as crews specializing in various fields would come and go, in sequence, as the renovation work progressed at various plants. For the first time in my life, I was truly experiencing the fruits of my hard work. The N&W contract coupled with the Reynolds plant renovation business was bringing a monthly cash flow that was more than my yearly salary at Nabisco, my first job as a research scientist.

One day in August 1980, at a lunch break, my colleagues at RJR Foods decided to visit me at Winkler. Jerry Bloumquist, Bob Appleyard, and Steve Kelly were area QA managers. Jerry was driving, Bob was in the front, and Steve was in the backseat. As they drove in the back entrance, they saw me coming up the hill with a toolbox in my left hand and a plunger in my right. Milan was standing outside the laundry room. Halfway down the hill, Jerry stopped, put the car in park, opened the door, and rushed over to me.

"What the hell are you doing? What are you doing with this toolbox?"

I said, "I had a few items to clear on the maintenance list."

He shouted, "And what is the plunger doing in your hand?"

"I have a commode to fix in Room 502."

"Bart, what the hell is going on? You're a PhD!"

The funny thing was that it was the same group that had helped me buy that toolbox when I became a new homeowner about seven years earlier!

Steve Kelley ran over to Milan and asked if we had enough food on the table for the family. Milan understood the question but was not sure how to answer.

Milan and I spent some time with them. We showed them some of the newly renovated rooms and calmed their fears about food on the family table. One thing I didn't tell them was that during the last three months at the Winkler, I had a cash flow that equaled my yearly salary at Reynolds.

The increase in revenue, coupled with tight control on property expenses, resulted in our savings account swelling. Milan and I had never seen this kind of money in our life as a married couple. Before Winkler, our yearly savings would be around $1,500, money I would receive as a tax refund at the end of the year. As promised to Jim Myers, our expenses at home, except for a little freedom on Mit's and Raj's clothes and toys, were also controlled. Come December 1980, I was prepared to pay off Jim Myers for the remaining down payment as well as money borrowed from friends. Jim was happy that we were doing so well. Betty Myers visited the property and was happy to see that we were keeping it in good condition. I had borrowed from friends at 10 percent interest.

I paid each one 12 percent interest to cover their shortfall if they had pulled out the money to loan me from a long-term savings account. Except for the mortgages on home and Winkler, the Shah family was debt free!

It was time to celebrate financial freedom!

Chapter 17
The First Family Vacation

My father had done very well financially in 1957, and he took the entire family, along with the chauffeur and the chef, on vacation all the way to the valleys of Kashmir. For us, the children, it was the first and the best family outing ever. Following in his footsteps, I was ready for a family vacation, too.

We planned three weeks of travel on Delta Airlines during December 1980. Mitesh, who we called Mit, was eleven, and Rajesh, who we called, Raj, was seven; this was their first vacation. Our itinerary included Bermuda, the Bahamas, New York, San Francisco, Los Angeles, and San Diego. *The Mobil Travel Guide* was our reference book. Regardless of the price, we wanted to stay at the best hotels and dine at the best restaurants.

We left Greensboro for Atlanta around December 20, 1980. Mit had a cassette player with a mic and kept an oral diary of our travels, narrating the details of our changing location. Our first stop was Bermuda. We stayed at a beautiful resort on the top of a mountain overlooking the Atlantic Ocean. The rooms and restaurants were in two separate buildings, with a large swimming pool in between. The breakfast buffet was elaborate—we had never seen anything like it in our lives. Returning to our rooms after the buffet, as we were passing the pool, Mit and Raj began shoving each other. All of a sudden, Raj was in deep water. He didn't know how to swim. Completely clothed, I jumped into the pool and pulled him out. That was our first day of vacation, and we weren't getting off to a good start. A little scared ourselves, both Milan and I gave the guys lectures on discipline.

The next stop was the Bahamas. We stayed at the Holiday Inn at Paradise Island in the Bahamas. On the first evening, we gave some money to the boys and told them to eat at whichever restaurant at the hotel complex they wanted. Milan and I went to a seafood restaurant within the hotel complex. After dinner we all got together for entertainment in the lobby, where various dancers and singers presented a show. When it was over, around midnight, we walked up to an elevator lobby to return to our room. As we waited for the elevator, Milan realized she was missing her purse! The purse had our passports, tickets, and a large amount of cash and traveler's checks. We asked Mit and Raj to stay right there, and Milan and I rushed to the lobby. We looked around the sofa where we had been sitting but didn't find the purse. The next stop was the seafood restaurant, which we had left three hours before. Both of us were really scared, thinking about possibly not finding the purse anywhere. Just as we reached the restaurant, gasping for air, a security staff member asked us if we were the Shahs. We said yes. The waiter who served us had found the purse. A security officer asked Milan to check the contents of the purse to make sure that all the cash was there. Milan found everything intact. I offered a hundred-dollar tip to the waiter, and he respectfully declined. Every place was giving us a new experience—some good and some definitely not so good.

We spent the next two days in an elaborate pool, on the beach, and doing some shopping. We went to a local fruit market and bought mango, guava, and sugarcane. Milan loved guavas, which we usually did not find in the States. She packed whatever was left into a suitcase to consume during the next few days. The next morning we headed for the airport on our way to Atlanta. At the airport, the US customs officer asked, "Are you carrying any fruits or vegetables with you?"

Milan, the spokesperson for the family, answered, "No."

Raj heard the answer and burst out, "But, Mom—"

Before Raj could finish the statement, Milan told him in Gujarati to shut up. He did.

The officer asked Milan again, "Ma'am, are you carrying any fruits or vegetables?"

Milan's answer was an emphatic, "No."

We were allowed to proceed further without checking any bags. A new rule was established on the tarmac before getting on the plane. Milan gave a strict warning, especially to Raj, not to say a word if an officer asked any questions in future. "I'll handle all of that—no one else!" That was the order from the chief!

Our next stop was New York. Our sightseeing included the Statue of Liberty, Rockefeller Center, and a music show at the Radio City Music Hall. Two days later, we were in San Francisco.

Many of my colleagues from RJR Foods had moved to Walnut Creek, a suburb of San Francisco, when the company merged with Del Monte Foods. I had contacted a few friends there before leaving Winston-Salem. They were anxious to see me, and I was interested in finding out what I had missed by venturing into the hotel business. Don Harris was a director of purchasing for RJR Foods in Winston-Salem. Don, his wife, Betty, and their two sons lived in a beautiful, traditional house in Buena Vista, the best neighborhood in Winston-Salem. Most of our Friday night poker games were played there. Betty was a happy housewife with a couple of housemaids to do the chores. Don and I had traveled together to the Texas coast and to Oklahoma to find American sources for shrimp and mung beans for the Chun King brand products. One evening, while we were in San Francisco, we were invited to have dinner at Don's house in Walnut Creek. When we got there at seven in the evening, Don was home, waiting for us. Betty had not arrived from work yet. Why was Betty working? The new mortgage payment was too high, and Betty had to work to make up the shortfall. The house was about one-third the size of their palatial home in Winston-Salem, and the neighborhood was nothing compared to Buena Vista. Don wasn't a happy camper, and Betty looked tired when she reached home. And from what Don and Betty told us, a lot of my old colleagues were in similar situations. I told my story, and both of them were genuinely happy for us. One would see this as a coincidence but in my own heart I saw it a blessing, a miracle, that my timing to leave RJR Foods came at an exact moment when Winkler provided a stable financial base with an upward momentum compared to my colleagues. I felt a great deal of gratitude towards god when I looked at Milan, Mit, and Raj and thought about our good life together as how happy and content we were together.

The next stop was Los Angeles. After Disneyland and Knott's Berry Farm, we were at Universal Studios on New Year's Day, 1981. As the family was standing in line to buy tickets, I found a public phone to call the Winkler. Donna was the manager in charge. I wanted to know how we had done on New Year's Eve. During the day, some people had checked out early. Those rooms were redone by the housekeeping staff and were rented again. Our ninety-unit property had sold 117 rooms that night for 130 percent occupancy. I was very happy and asked Donna to keep up the good work. It was really a Happy New Year!

Bharat & Milan

The next stop was San Diego to visit Sea World. After a couple of days in San Diego, we made a quick trip to Tijuana before we would head back home.

On our way back in the US from Mexico, we stood in the immigration line with Milan's and my passports in hand. Mit and Raj were included in my passport. When we got to the front of the line, the officer looked at Raj and asked him,

"Son, where do you live?"

Raj looked everywhere but at the officer and didn't answer.

The officer asked the question again, and Raj behaved as if he didn't understand the English language.

Perhaps thinking we were trying to smuggle a Mexican boy across the border, the officer looked at me and asked, "Sir, who's this kid?"

I replied, "Sir, he's my son,"

Suddenly I realized what was going on: it was the strict warning Milan had drilled into him while leaving the Bahamas. Raj was just following orders. I blurted out, "Rajya, speak up: Where are you from?"

He let it out in one burst: "3018 Loch Drive, Winston-Salem, North Carolina."

The officer smiled, and we were back in the United States, safe and sound, on our way home. Again, one of the best family vacations of my life, and this time it was with my children—their first!

Just as my sisters, brother Sanjay and I had enjoyed our first family vacation in Kashmir during the summer of 1957 and the way the foundation of our family bond was laid, this next generation of the Shah Family had continued the legacy with fond memories to last a lifetime.

CHAPTER 18

My Calling— Community Work

As a boy, I often observed my father running campaigns for political candidates. He had a large contingent of volunteers who basically lived at our home, handling errands as requested. He had private meetings with these candidates who listened to him regarding the most important issues the people were facing and followed his advice in order to win. Pappa was known as the Kingmaker, the godfather, for the county and state elections. I knew politics ran in my blood. Having achieved the status of a successful businessman, and belonging to the Winston-Salem Chamber of Commerce and the Convention and Visitors Bureau, I decided it was time to get involved. In 1980, we were in an election year and I read about a fundraising event for the Democratic Party. That evening I went to the house where the event was being held. As I entered the door, I saw a few serious-looking men and women, most of them white, a couple of them black. I was the only Asian at the small gathering. Before I got any further, a white gentleman greeted me and thanked me for coming. His name was Robert Joyce, and he was a Democratic Party coordinator for Winston-Salem. I told him my name and that I owned the Winkler Motor Inn, on Peters Creek Parkway. It just happened that Robert's father had an auto license plate office across from Winkler. He knew Jim Myers and his family. With this kind of family connection, we hit it off right away. Immediately he took me to see a gentleman and told him, "Governor, I want you to meet Bart Shah. He owns a motel in town just across from my dad's tag office." I was being introduced to Governor Jim Hunt of North Carolina. He was a very pleasant, down-to-earth man. He thanked me for coming and being a supporter of the Democratic Party. Robert knew that Winkler had a long frontage on Peters Creek Parkway. He asked me if I would allow the candidates' signs to be placed on the frontage. Without hesitation I said, "By all means." The governor was very happy. He and I hit it off very well, too, and we talked for a long time. He addressed me as "Bart." I had carried a checkbook, and I asked Robert for the amount of check he thought I should write. I wrote a check for one hundred dollars to the Democratic party of North Carolina, my entry fee into the political arena of the United States of America! Within a week Winkler's entrance and street frontage were dotted with the signs of various Democratic party candidates. Winston-Salem and the state of North Carolina leaned more toward the Democrats during the eighties. Overnight, I became a hero among city officials and other leaders in Winston-Salem. Jim Myers was also a Democrat, and he loved my involvement in local politics when he visited Winkler.

Robert Joyce and I became good friends. I would join him for any political event and financially support candidates he recommended. In return I got a favorable reception at any city or county office when I needed any license or permit for work at Winkler. I didn't even need to stand in line; many times the paperwork was delivered right to me. One summer morning in 1982, I received a call from my friend Babu Patel from Greensboro. He was also a motel owner. He informed me that many motel owners with the last name "Patel" had received letters from their insurance companies that their property and liability insurance coverage was canceled, effective immediately. Babu had a network of friends nationwide, and he told me that Patels in several states received similar letters. This sounded very odd. I went to Greensboro and met with my friends. There were about eight Patels in the area that had lost insurance coverage. What we learned was that in the state of Mississippi, a couple of motel owners by the last name Patel had burned their properties to claim damage coverage. Upon investigation, they were charged with arson and fraud. The insurance companies, through their internal networking, took a unilateral action throughout the country. Almost all Indian hoteliers with the last name Patel lost their property insurance overnight. It was as if one Patel was bad, then all the Patels were bad. This was totally unreasonable and discriminatory. I returned to Winston-Salem and called Robert. He was quick to understand the reason for my call and asked me if I wanted to see the governor. I said yes; I knew we had to go to the highest level possible to get anything done.

Within two days a contingent of about twenty Indians, with Robert Joyce as our captain, left for Raleigh to meet the honorable Governor Jim Hunt.

The governor came out of his office to greet us and led us to a board-room. Many of my friends who joined us from Greensboro had never met an elected official, much less the governor of a state. Robert presented the basic reason for our visit and thanked the governor for meeting with us on such a short notice. He then asked me to elaborate. I gave the details on the insurance cancellations and expressed our collective fear of being sued by someone, which would result in a major financial loss. The governor turned to his assistant, Betty, and asked her to see if the insurance commissioner, Jim Ingram, was in his office. He told her that if the commissioner was in the office, she was to ask him to come to the governor's boardroom immediately. Within the next twenty minutes, Jim Ingram arrived. The governor introduced us as friends of the Democratic Party and turned to me to explain the situation to the commissioner. I repeated my story, and as soon as I finished, the governor asked, "Commissioner, what do you think of the situation? Don't you think this is a case of discrimination?"

The commissioner answered, "Yes, sir, it is."

Then another question: "Then what do you think your office can do?"

The commissioner replied, "Sir, we'll take care of it."

I was watching the scene as it was unfolding. A group of immigrants, with hardly any financial contribution to the political machinery, were receiving honest and fair treatment in a foreign land. This was our land of freedom and opportunity! United States of America!

The commissioner asked if he could leave. As he was leaving, we all got up to thank him, not knowing what exactly he had in mind. The governor asked us all to sit down, and then he asked me, "Bart, do you have an association?"

I said, "No, sir."

He exclaimed: "No man is an island"!

Then he gave us a lesson in the reality of politics. He advised us to form an association because, in this American democratic world, only numbers count. Individuals cannot fight major issues the way we had just tried to do. We all took the advice to heart and left for Greensboro after thanking him and Robert Joyce.

Jim Ingram, the insurance commissioner for the state of North Carolina, came through on his promise. Within one week all of our North Carolina friends whose insurance had been canceled received letters from their respective insurance companies, stating their insurance policies were being reinstated without any lapse of coverage. Each letter had a statement of apology for any inconvenience that their action may have caused. All around the nation, from California to New York, we learned many Patels lost their property insurance coverage. California residents tried to form their own insurance company; in Tennessee some tried to form insurance cooperatives; and others just settled for allowing the insurance companies to charge higher premiums for the same coverage as before cancellation. We in North Carolina, got the insurance policies reinstated promptly and without hassle.

We took Governor Hunt's recommendation to form our own association seriously and immediately initiated the planning. The most active community leaders were Babu Patel, Sitaram Dakoria, Dhansukh Panwala, Jagdish Dhekar, Manu Patel, and Diamond Patel. We hired Panwala's attorney in High Point to write the constitution and bylaws for the newly formed group. The charter named the group the India Merchants Association. Anyone of Indian origin, having a business interest, could become a member. I had a strong bond and affection with the Indian community of Greensboro. While my friends had tremendous respect for my work on behalf of our community, I was simply eager to help achieve our common goals with the right perspective. I was asked to become the founding president of India Merchants Association, and I accepted the honor. For a few months thereafter, we were on the road all over North Carolina and to bordering towns in South Carolina and Virginia. When we were done, the membership roster reached nearly two hundred Indians.

Motel owners, convenience store owners, gas station owners, and even doctors were among the members. It quickly became a thriving business association in central North Carolina. We held membership meetings on the last Thursday of each month. We invited speakers to teach us about tax laws, estate planning, and other business topics. Dinner was served at the end of the meeting. I remained, or was forced to remain, the president of India Merchants Association for the next five years, until Milan pleaded to send her husband home!

It was a middle of a wintery night in January of 1983. I received a call from a friend in Greensboro that six Indian hoteliers from Greensboro–High Point area had been picked up by an immigrations officer and were taken to federal prison. The immigrations officer was heard saying that he was after many more illegal immigrants like these, and that night's raid was the first one of many to follow. The word was that the informant was from our own Indian community. The man worked as a desk clerk at one of the motels owned by an Indian and was jealous of the progress others were making. It was believed that he kept a diary of all the illegal in the community.

I woke up Robert Joyce that night and filled him in on the scenario. He told me he would contact a few people and get back to me. Robert called me back around four in the morning; he had tracked down the group. They were at a federal prison in Winston-Salem. Robert had contacted the head jailor and asked him to take good care of his "friends." The next morning we were at the immigration court in Charlotte for the hearing. Meanwhile, Robert had contacted North Carolina fifth district US senator, Steve Neal, who was a Democrat and a resident of Winston-Salem. Senator Neal did two things for us. He contacted the State Department in Washington, DC, and had the immigration officer stopped from making any more raids. He also contacted the Charlotte court judge and had each of the defendants released on his or her own recognizance, without any bonds or bail.

We learned for the first time that our community had a number of families who were illegal in this country. I had played tennis with RJR corporate attorney Gary Avram when I was at Reynolds. I made a phone call to Gary and asked him to recommend a top-notch immigration attorney. He did his research and in few days gave me the name of David Carlyle, in Washington, DC. David handled Reynolds's personnel cases related to immigration status. Gary had discussed our need with David and had told him to expect a call from me. When I called David Carlyle, he was friendly; sincerely interested in helping anyone with a genuine need—and, most importantly, money was not an issue. After a few conversations, we came up with a plan that David would come early on a Sunday morning to Greensboro and would meet individually with as many families as he could until the last flight out that day to Washington. On our end, we were to buy his ticket, pay his fee of $3,000, and provide a cup of masala tea anytime he needed one. I discussed the plan with my friends in Greensboro. The India Merchants Association made an announcement and asked a few families who had their own networks to spread the word. We asked all the families to bring any and all credentials for all their family members. We decided to charge a one-hundred-dollar fee to each family meeting David, and the India Merchants Association would make up the shortfall. The word was spread very quickly among the members of the association. We learned that there were a lot of families who needed help. We had taken up a very worthwhile cause for the good of the community.

We met David at the Greensboro airport on a Sunday morning. He was a simple man, carrying a worn leather briefcase and dressed very casually. We stopped for a light breakfast on the way to our gathering place, Sitaram Dakoria's Best Western Inn on Lee Street in Greensboro. A crowd of about 150 people were waiting for us. Some were there for consultation and others as helpers in case we needed them. We set up a special room for the meeting. Babu Patel and other friends coordinated the families to form an orderly process. David would discuss the general situation with the parents, then look at each child's birth certificate and certification of any special training, especially in the medical field. I sat as an interpreter for questions from both sides. David would suggest ways to apply for resident alien status. The family could use that advice or go to any attorney to apply for immigration. At the end of the day, before catching a nine o'clock flight, David had spoken to nearly thirty families. There was no lunch break, only Indian masala tea breaks every couple of hours. The end result was that almost all of the families had some valid credential or background in order to legally apply for residency status.

Today, when I visit Greensboro and its surrounding towns, I see those families well settled. The young children who sat with their parents have grown to be professionals in various fields, married with their own children. Thirty years have passed since then, and my contribution to the well-being of my community still remains a personal pride for me. Unknown to me and without any expectations, I believe, the seeds of good deeds were sown and the fruits awaited in the future.

CHAPTER 19
Family Growth in Real Estate

After almost ten years of struggle to enter a business world, a real estate opportunity had knocked at the Shah's door in the form of the Winkler Motor Inn. RAAM Corporation was formed to acquire the Winkler. *RA* was derived from Rang Avdhut, my spiritual guru from Nareshvar. *AM* was derived from the goddess Amba, representing Milan's family deity. RAAM Corporation was the mother of all the business entities that followed thereafter.

The cash flow generated from the Winkler's operation was unbelievable, considering the income level we had achieved during the previous decade. Real estate tax laws that allowed depreciation deductions and investment tax credits on the amount allotted to equipment and machinery reduced our tax bill to almost zero. Over and above, we received refunds on taxes paid during my last three years at RJR. The first step was to pay off the loans taken from friends and the remaining balance on the down payment I owed Jim Myers. Our next priority was to continue investing in real estate. Consultations with our accountants resulted in our strategy to invest in apartment complexes. In the early 1980's, investments in apartments did not generate much cash flow but provided a good tax shelter because of the depreciation deductions that could be put against the hotel cash flow.

Milan and I began driving around Winston-Salem and neighboring communities, looking for an attractive property to purchase. As I look back, our process seemed so primitive. Instead of doing a blind search ourselves, we could have hired a real estate broker to do a search, and then we could have selected the right property for an investment. But we didn't know any better; we'd never been down this path before. One evening we were searching a neighborhood a mile from our home called Oldtown. Yarbrough Avenue in Oldtown had plenty of good-looking apartment complexes lined up one after another. We stopped in front of a well-lit, nicely landscaped apartment complex named St. Armand's and marveled at its good looks. Milan and I both thought we wouldn't be able to afford it. One afternoon, Milan went to St. Armand's and talked to the resident manager. She got the phone numbers for the owners, Troy and Vonnie Woods. When she called, Troy picked up the phone, and after some conversation he said the apartments weren't for sale. Vonnie overheard the conversation, grabbed the phone from Troy, and told Milan they were for sale. We finalized the price and down payment after a few meetings and convinced the Woods to carry the mortgage. During the middle of August 1982, we became the owners of the most beautiful apartment complex in the area. I would spend the day at Winkler and go to St. Armand's in the evening. A couple of hours in the office was enough to meet with tenants as needed, collect the rent, and make a list of maintenance needs. All the tenants, black and white, were professionals working at RJR, Wachovia, Hanes, and various hospitals in Winston-Salem. There was some minor renovation work needed, such as painting the building and fixing the wooden rails, which was done immediately. The monument sign in the front got completely redone with a new logo I coined for St. Armand's: "Neighborhood of Nice People."

Milan continued to look for more investments, mainly in the apartment rental business. Through her own research, she located Starlight Apartments, an eleven-acre complex, with fifty-four one-bedroom apartments and a four-thousand-square-foot stone house. The house had four bedrooms, a carved ceiling, and a stone fireplace in the living room. The pool that went with the house was the largest private pool in the city, fed by an artesian well, but it was closed for unattended repairs. The complex had been the homestead of the president of the Royal Cake Company and his family before the present owner developed it for a commercial use. During the spring of 1984, we acquired the Starlight Apartments with a cash down payment and took over the existing mortgage. Our friend Bhagu Panchal and his wife, Saroj, moved to Winston-Salem from India in the mid 1980's. Bhagu, a medical professional, got a job with Forsyth

Hospital. We hired Saroj to manage the Starlight, and they became the resident managers.

During the late 80's, Latino immigrants began to move into the area, and more and more were becoming tenants. I maintained my routine of being at the St. Armand's office in the evening. During the latter part of one month, there was a knock on the office door. I shouted, "Come in." A large Latino family entered. I asked in slow English if there was any problem. Very sheepishly the man said, "Señor, we want to pay the rent." Rent in advance for the next month. I accepted the rent with pleasure and asked them to bring in any of their countrymen looking for an apartment to rent. My mind traveled back to 1970 when I was a tenant at Tivoli Gardens Apartments in Parsippany, New Jersey. Just to be a good tenant, I would take my rent check in advance. At first the resident manager was apprehensive of my knocking on his door at night. A few visits thereafter he would ask me to come in. He would serve me coffee and then request me to bring my countrymen looking for an apartment to rent. Twenty years later, I was a landlord, and an immigrant tenant was following the same routine that I had followed as a tenant. What a beautiful experience! Later on, as I got involved in other properties and activities, I hired Kenny and Beverley Strickland to manage St. Armand's. The operation went on with its ups and downs of occupancy without any fanfare.

Both apartments ran very well for a couple of years. St. Armand's was the place to be in the Oldtown neighborhood and Starlight was mostly occupied because businesses like Royal Cake, Westinghouse, and Schlitz Brewery provided a good tenant base. However, when new competition came in a few years later, the business climate changed. For the first time ever, I started seeing vacancies at both St. Armand's and Starlight.

President Ronald Reagan's new tax law of 1986 dealt a strong blow to apartment investments relative to a tax shelter. Hotel operations were qualified as an active investment, whereas apartment operations were now considered a passive investment. Beginning in 1986, the losses from the apartment business were not allowed to offset profits from our hotel operations. Though Schlitz Brewery closed and the Royal Cake Company ran into financial problems, Starlight never became a monetary burden on us.

However, lower occupancy at St. Armand's resulted in actual cash loss to us without providing any tax benefit. After nearly twenty years as owners, we sold both the apartments for close to what we paid for them. Looking back, I did not feel that our investment in rental properties was financially worthwhile considering the hassle and headache that came with it.

In 1984, RJR Tobacco Company made an announcement that it would develop a cigarette manufacturing plant in Tobacoville, a small town about fifteen miles north of Winston-Salem. The plant would be the largest in the world, producing sixteen thousand cigarettes per minute per machine. The plant would be a showcase of robotics; no human being would touch any cigarette component. We visited the King/Tobacoville township to build a sixty-unit Econo Lodge that would cater to the new demand. Within a few weeks, we bought a three-acre parcel for $120,000 in an all-cash transaction.

When we lived in New Jersey, Amrut and Sumati Lala had been close friends of ours. They were the ones who had opened their home and their hearts to us when Milan and I, a newly married couple, had just arrived in the United States. When we moved to North Carolina, the Lalas had moved to Texas, where Amrut was a plant manager for an ink company. We remained in touch. Amrut eventually resigned from his job because the plant environment was hazardous to his health. When we talked about a new hotel project in King, they asked us to take them on as partners. We did not need any financial help or operational help in developing the project. Milan and I were contributing a larger share of cash equity and we were the only ones who signed the personal guarantee for the loan. We brought the Lalas in as equal partners. I, in my own heart, was returning a favor extended to me fifteen years earlier when the Lalas kindness helped Milan and I get settled in the United States.

During that time, Marty Cope of Rock Hill, South Carolina, was a hotel builder of good reputation. He was building a Comfort Inn for another Shah family in Rock Hill. Milan and I visited the project under construction. We met Dr. Jugal Shah, a cardiologist, and his wife, Leena, the owners of the project. Our two families became good friends and have remained very close ever since. Marty built the sixty-unit Econo Lodge for us in King, an all-brick building with a kidney-shaped pool right in front. It was the new age of limited service hotels and we were very proud owners.

It was summer of 1986 and my parents had just arrived from India on their second visit to the States. My father had won the Sagbara case in the Supreme Court of Gujarat. However, the judgment was skewed in that the court awarded only eight cents to a dollar as compensation, reasoning that the rules had changed such that the trees could not be cut anymore. Pappa had lost twenty four years of his life fighting the government and he was a tired and a broken man. He accepted the verdict and brought money home. He personally went to each and every lender and paid what he owed with full interest. At the end, very little money was left for their living expenses. I was informed by my cousin Rajnibhai of the Sagbara settlement and financial situation at home. When Pappa and I were by ourselves, he gave me the details of the settlement and that he had paid everybody, not mentioning of what was left over. I asked him how much were the family's living expense per year. When he mentioned the amount, I told him that I would send double the amount for him and mother to live the rest of their lives in the luxury that they had when I was a child. His eyes sparkled as he accepted my gesture.

At the opening of the Econo Lodge, the town leaders were delighted in our confidence and commitment to build a million-dollar property. We were the first major business at that interstate and Milan had selected the furniture, fixtures, and decorations. It turned out so beautifully that the townsfolk named it the Mini-Hilton. I had made contact with King's city office and had invited the mayor for the opening. I had my father cut the ribbon in the presence of city officials, prominent business owners, and friends. He was a proud man to see his son become a successful businessman in a foreign land.

Amrut was a good manager and managed the property professionally. He was very conscious of expenses and kept a tight lid on them. The occupancy increased gradually, and within six months, the bottom line was in the black. Over the years, the property received seven national awards at the Econo Lodge annual conference. Their parent company was so impressed with our housekeeping procedures that the director of QA had a company camera crew come and take a video of our entire process. Our head housekeeper, Arlene, was the star performer. The Lalas operated the Econo Lodge for almost twenty years before we sold the property. Still today, the property looks brand new.

Spartanburg County, South Carolina, was one of the fastest growing counties in the nation during the mid-1980s. A large BMW plant was to be built between the cities of Spartanburg and Greenville. One day I received a call from Mohanbhai. He had moved to Daytona Beach, Florida, from Johannesburg, South Africa, and had acquired several hotel properties over the years. Mohanbhai asked me to look into the prospects in the Spartanburg area and expressed a desire to develop a property in partnership. After researching the area, we contacted Bill Williams of Williams Realty in Spartanburg to help us find a hotel site in the county. We arrived in Spartanburg, and Bill took us all around the city and beyond. At the end of the day, when I asked him which parcel he thought was the best location for a hotel, he took us to exit 63 on Interstate 85. The location was three miles from the BMW plant. It was within the city limits of Duncan, South Carolina. After taking a few months to determine the feasibility of the project and make a decision, we acquired a three-acre parcel near the interstate exit and received approval for a Comfort Inn franchise.

South Carolina National Bank was more than happy to make the loan. The bank asked the two partners, Mohanbhai and me, to bring our financial statements for the loan approval process. I called Mohanbhai in Daytona Beach and planned for our trip to Spartanburg. On the morning of the meeting, I drove from Winston-Salem and picked up Mohanbhai at Spartanburg-Greenville airport. When we reached the parking lot of the bank, I opened the car trunk to take our briefcases out. I wanted to be well informed for our presentation, so I carefully asked Mohanbhai how many properties he had. He looked a little puzzled. "Bharatbhai, don't take this wrong, but I really don't know the number. It's somewhere in the fifties." I said to myself, *Oh my God. I'm doing a second hotel property, and my partner has more than fifty, and what a humble answer!* The disparity between our portfolios became even more apparent when he pulled out his financial statements.

The stack was at least two inches thick; mine was two pages. The bank officer did not even look at my financial statements. We walked out in less than thirty minutes with the loan approved.

Bharat with Mohanbhai

The eighty-unit property construction started in the spring of 1987. Before we got ready to open the property, Milan trained the housekeepers, and Raj, who at fourteen was out of school for the summer, trained the desk staff. Raj was a great teacher for the computer-based desk training. Whenever we would leave back to Winston-Salem, the front desk staff missed Raj the most. Milan would often stay in Winston-Salem to look after Winkler and the apartment complexes. Raj and I would go to Spartanburg and stay there to oversee construction, train personnel, and get ready for the opening. A couple of weeks before the opening of the hotel, I felt Raj needed a good vacation. I planned a trip to Gatlinburg, Tennessee, and the two of us left for a well-deserved break. Spending time in the Smoky Mountains for four days was a great bonding experience for our father-and-son team. It remains one of my fondest memories.

Eventually, the Econo Lodge franchise was bought by Choice Hotels International. Choice also had the Comfort Inn and Comfort Suites brands in its portfolio. Milan and I went for a three-day management training to learn how to run a Comfort Inn. During the training on housekeeping, we were asked to watch their prescribed process on "How to Clean a Room." As the training video started, I recognized the Econo Lodge building in King. Then our superstar Arlene came on the screen! We were watching our own housekeeping process, which Choice Hotels had picked up from the Econo Lodge franchise. We opened the Comfort Inn in the summer of 1988, the first hotel at the exit—and in the town of Duncan. We invited many dignitaries, bank officers, and local business owners for the grand opening. Mohanbhai arrived from Daytona Beach. The mayor of Duncan cut the ribbon. I acknowledged Mohanbhai for encouraging me to get into the hotel business. As we were standing in the lobby, the mayor's wife asked me the name of our interior decorator. Apparently she was very impressed with the color scheme, the selection of decorative articles in the lobby, and the furniture and fixtures in the rooms. I pointed to the interior decorator, Milan, who was standing next to me. The two ladies became inseparable.

From the day it opened, the Comfort Inn made a good profit. I kept a good watch on the operations through property managers. By 2005, there were more properties built on the exit on I-85. As new competition arrived, a twenty-year-old Comfort Inn lost business, and we started losing money. A year later we sold it. I learned through the school of hard knocks that this is the real estate business. You have to know when to hold and profit but also when to fold and sell when the time is right.

By 1988, Milan and I decided to concentrate only on our hotels. The hotel properties generated good cash flow year after year. We had planned to sell the older properties and perhaps invest in new markets like the Raleigh and Greensboro airports; Charlotte; and Columbia, South Carolina. All the mortgages on our hotels and apartments would soon be paid in full. We would have generated a lot of cash flow by selling some of the locations and holding on to others that still had a profitable performance. The recession that started in the late 1980's and through the early 1990's jolted the family yet again. However, our family net worth had increased significantly from where we had started and Milan and I knew we had our eventual retirement covered well.

When Milan and I became US citizens in 1978, our wish was to sponsor our siblings to come to the United States as immigrants. I sponsored my sisters, Saryu, Kunju, Malini and all of their family members.

My baby sister, Malini, arrived first in 1981 with her husband Samir and young sons, Kaushal and Niraj. Through the years, Malini became a well regarded high school teacher in Passaic, NJ. Samir is a successful real estate agent. Kaushal and Niraj are professionals in information technology and corporate management. Elder Kaushal is married to Sudhin, a medical professional in New York city, and they have an year old son, Ethan. Samir and Malini built a good life together in the United States as wonderful parents and now grandparents.

My older sister Saryu and husband Chandrakant arrived in US in 1986 and moved with their son Sunil in Glendale, California. Sunil had married Rashmi in 1983 and had arrived in California where Rashmi was a management professional. Sunil's younger brother Sandip arrived in 1987 and married Mita in 1994. Together, the brothers have built a family business with multiple dry cleaning operations and are well established. Both the brothers have grown-up children. Sunil's son, Neel, is married to Sonam and daughter Nisha is married to Arun. Both the couples are professionals and well settled. Sandip's son Raj and daughter Richa are in school. United States has helped to realize a wonderful destiny for Saryu and Malini's families.

My sister Kunju and husband Vinesh had come to the United States as immigrants. However, as much as Vinesh's construction business was succeeding in Surat, they did not see a need to leave India and start life all over. Kunju and her daughters Dipti, Trupti, Shruti and Shital remain well settled in Surat, India.

My mother passed away in 1994 as a result of complication of severe diabetes. I had rushed to Navapur to attend the cremation ceremony. Pappa was doing well with the help of a housekeeper and a care taker at home. However, within a year, he had fallen sick and was hospitalized in Surat. We then brought him back home to Navapur where we looked after him and tried to feed him his favorite food dishes. I was with my father the day he passed away and held his hand as he took his last breath. The trustees of the Dattatraya temple were informed of my father's death. As per his instructions, the key to the Navapur house was given back to the head trustee. By their grace, Manubhai Diwan's family lived in the house, donated by Dr. Bhangrej, for more than sixty years.

CHAPTER 20
Noble Investment Group

When we made our entry into the hospitality business with the purchase of Winkler Motor Inn, Mit was ten years old, and Raj was six. From the very beginning, I was taking Mit to Winkler every Saturday and Sunday to help me with the 7a.m. to 3p.m. first shift. The kid was smart, and he could handle hotel operations. One hot summer day in 1979, Mit needed money to pay for a Boy Scout outing. I asked him to take care of the vending machines after the shift to earn the cash. We formed a partnership; I provided the opportunity and Mit did the work. For that, he received 50 percent of the profits. He used some of his income for things he wanted to buy on his own, but most of it went into his account at a brokerage house. He handled his own portfolio with a broker friend I had contacted for him. A few months later, I taught him the hotel budget process and made him understand the importance of the bottom line. I showed him how the five-year pro forma was created, the numbers a bank would want to see before a loan approval. He understood it well and loved playing with the numbers. What he didn't enjoy was the other hotel-related chores, like cleaning rooms, picking up towels from the laundry room and distributing them to various rooms and delivering supplies to the housekeepers and the maintenance man. Raj was four years younger than Mit. In a few years, I started bringing him with me to the Winkler as well. I was a little softer on Raj and gave him a choice of working on either Saturday or Sunday. He loved the hotel business when his big brother was at the desk. He could get the vending machine key and get as many sodas as he wanted of all different varieties. Raj went through the same training on budget and finance, and he was also good with numbers.

When the Comfort Inn in Spartanburg, South Carolina, was under construction in 1988, I visited the site many times and left Mit to look after the Winkler and St. Armand's. By then, Mit was a freshman at Wake Forest University in Winston-Salem. He would arrive at the properties after his classes and make sure things were running smoothly. One afternoon I arrived early from Spartanburg and decided to run by the Winkler. As I was entering the lobby area, I heard Mit giving strict instructions to the maintenance man to have the parking lot cleaned in the next thirty minutes before a large group of guests arrived. I had spent the whole year with the same man, requesting him to clean the parking lot "when he found time." Some days he found time, some days he didn't. I turned around, went to my car, and drove home. Winkler was in much better hands than mine!

Mit graduated from Wake Forest University in 1991 with a Bachelor's degree in finance and economics. I believed I had run him ragged running the Winkler while he was growing up. He showed no interest in joining the family business. His passion was numbers and to join an investment banking firm. In 1991, the job environment he found himself in was similar to the ones I experienced when I graduated from UT Knoxville and Utah State in the 1960's. During his four years at Wake Forest, Mit had worked at an executive conference center managed by Marriott International. Mit worked in many different positions and departments and got professional experience in operations and food service. He developed a great rapport with Marriott corporate executives who offered him a management staff position in Denver. Through his summer internships, he was also offered an opportunity to join the management training program at Centura Bank, which later became RBC Centura, in Rocky Mount, North Carolina. He was also approached for a finance position at a start-up investment bank called Thomas Financial in Atlanta. Mit asked me for my advice, and I told him I knew he would enjoy finance more than hotel operations. And as my father had guided me, I relayed to my son that he would have more opportunity to grow personally and professionally outside the comfort of his current environment. Mit accepted the position in Atlanta with Thomas Financial in 1991. His assignment was to analyze and prepare loan documents for real estate clients, many of whom had investments in the hospitality business.

Mit's work at Thomas Financial got him interested in learning about industries that were successful and the key traits that made them so. Mit began to develop a passion for entrepreneurial business models, especially those that could create sustainable cash flow. Because of Mit's operational understanding he learned in the family business from age ten and professionally with Marriott through college, he was chosen to be a key member of the team at Thomas Financial that led the underwriting and financing of a new product called limited service hotels. New hotel brands were being created such as Courtyard by Marriott, Hampton Inn and Holiday Inn Express that were purported to have eighty percent of the room rate of full service hotels but only fifty percent of the cost structure. Mit was intrigued by the profit potential of this new business model in hotel industry and was also fascinated by the emerging miniature golf course business. I knew my son had developed an entrepreneurial spirit, much as I had when I was his age. And I also knew that as my father had done for me, I was willing to put up the money to help him as best as I could when he was ready.

One day, Mohanbhai called me that he was visiting his friend Prakash Amin in Peachtree City, a small township forty-five minutes south of Atlanta. He asked that I join him. I took the opportunity to spend an entire day with a broker and surveyed metro Atlanta for existing putt-putt golf courses and some potential sites for a new development for Mit to enter his desired business enterprise. I went to Peachtree City in the evening to catch up with Mohanbhai at Prakash's home for dinner. As I entered Peachtree City, I was very impressed with the town's layout and landscaping. The town looked like a page out of a fairy-tale. I asked Prakash if he knew of any existing putt-putt golf courses in the town. He told me there were none, and he thought it would be a good business opportunity. He gave me a phone number of a friend, Pat Heaberg, director of Peachtree City Development Corporation (PCDC), for Mit to contact for further inquiry.

Mit went to see Pat Heaberg at his office along with his credentials. Pat noted that at the age of twenty-two, Mit had previously been a manager for a company known as RAAM Corporation in Winston-Salem, North Carolina. In their discussion, Pat asked Mit if his family was in the hotel business. Mit answered yes, they were. Pat advised Mit to put miniature golf on the side and to develop a Hampton Inn in Peachtree City. Pat said that for the last two years, the city's market research had identified a new hotel as the most needed development in town and they liked what the "new" Hampton Inn brand was selling. Mit called me after going through all the feasibility and financial information on the project to give me his thoughts on the opportunity. I was in Winston-Salem at the Winkler and facing the worst recession I had encountered to date. I was going through financial hardship, trying to make mortgage payments for the properties we had in our portfolio. But at the end of the conversation and without giving a thought about where the money would come from, I shouted, "Mit, let's do it!"

We took an option on a tract of land and were approved for a Hampton Inn franchise. The real challenge was to raise money, of which I had none, for the down payment for the construction of a $2.5 million project. I had kept good relationship with bank managers that we had accounts with and received commitment for a line of credit. We had some funds at the Comfort Inn in the money market, and I asked permission from Mohanbhai to use it. Our friends Jugal and Leena Shah came through with some help. The economy was so bad that I could not ask any of my other friends for a loan. Finally, I made contact with a loan shark who would lend to me at a very high interest rate. I never met the guy; I just needed the money, so I accepted his terms. Thus the down payment package was prepared. Peachtree National Bank, two blocks away from the construction site, was willing to provide an SBA loan, but they needed to see my financial statements. Mit arranged for a meeting and asked me to come to Atlanta with the required documents.

One morning in early 1993, I left Winston-Salem and picked up Mit from his office in Atlanta. When we reached the bank's parking lot, I pulled out my files from the car trunk. Just then, Mit asked me if I could let him do the talking. For a moment I was furious in my mind. For the last fifteen years, I had done the talking with brokers and banks, on behalf of myself and my fellow Indian motel owners. And here was this twenty-four year old Indian kid who wanted to talk to the bankers on my behalf, with my financials in his hands! Then I thought of my father, of what he would have done, and I received my answer: "Let the son do the talking."

"Are you sure, Mit?" I asked.

He replied, "Yes, Dad. Please."

I handed the files to him.

We walked inside the bank and were led to the boardroom. The bank president, branch manager, manager's secretary, and the loan officer were waiting for us. Mit sat next to the president, who was at the head of the table. I sat at a corner on the other end. As Mit presented the project details, the five-year pro forma, and the great viability of the project, I realized I couldn't have done it so well. I decided to zip my mouth until specifically asked to open it. Finally, the president spoke. He said he was very pleased with Mit's presentation, agreed to give us the loan, and was happy to have us as neighbors. Then he asked me, "Mr. Shah, I just want to know: where do you come in this picture?" I replied, "Sir, on page sixteen of this document, where you need the signature at the bottom, that's where I come in the picture." Everyone smiled. We shook hands and left the bank with a commitment to finance the hotel construction. The Hampton Inn construction began in March of 1993. Mit would be at the site every morning at 7am to meet with the project superintendent, making sure, on a daily basis, that the day's goals were met and that they had enough crew to do the work. He would then leave for his regular job at Thomas Financial in Atlanta. During one of my visits to Peachtree City, I realized that I didn't really understand the details of the blueprints thoroughly, even after building a couple of hotels. Mit had a thorough knowledge of it, and he made sure that the specifications were being met. The Hampton Inn in Peachtree City opened for business during the summer of 1994. The occupancy was great from day one. It was the only new property in town and the local community loved the product and the service they were provided.

One Thursday afternoon Mit called us at home in Winston-Salem to ascertain that we would be home over the coming weekend. He wished to discuss something, and he would arrive at the house late Friday night. We thought he had probably found a girl in Atlanta and wanted to talk to us about her. The morning after his arrival, we were at the breakfast table, and he asked me if he could look at my portfolio's financial statements. He told me that, working at Thomas Financial, he had looked at financial statements of Indian hoteliers who had a few properties, and the net worth of those individuals was substantial. Some of them could hardly speak English. At Thomas, Mit was on the team introducing a newly created commercial backed mortgage security (CMBS) instrument that would enable real estate owners to put long-term fixed debt on real estate assets and take out substantially all of their equity in the process. Who would have known how significant that product would become in the hospitality industry?

"Why do you want to look at my portfolio?" I asked, more curious than anything else.

"With the built-in equity of your properties, I believe we could re-finance and create some liquidity. I would like to create a company that would invest that cash in limited service hotel development."

I reminded him that at one point he had been done with the hotel business. He assured me that with what he had seen, it was indeed a good business, and he wanted to get involved. Milan and I were happy to hear that; however, this meant that we would start a new mortgage cycle for the properties we had developed during the 1980s. This also meant that most of our net worth was put at risk again. I had done that before when I bought the Winkler in 1979. I was forty years old then; I could have handled financial hardship or even a disaster much easier. I could have even gone back to work for Reynolds. This current scenario was more risky, considering that I was in my mid-fifties, the properties would have been paid off in four or five years and I was less likely to withstand another financial disaster. In recent years I have been interviewed by many trade and cultural magazines for my life story. Whenever I mentioned what transpired that day, the interviewers asked me whether I was in a right frame of mind. Why would anyone take a risk of this proportion, especially at the stage of life I was in? I can only say that I was euphoric, realizing that my elder son was entering the family business; and as a father I wanted to do whatever it took to help enable his path to be the most successful. As a matter of fact, the thought never occurred to me that I was gambling and could lose everything. I believe I was in the right frame of mind. However, I cannot claim it for sure.

Pretty soon, we developed a second Hampton Inn in the town of Newnan, Georgia. Soon, Mit had recognized the potential to build a scalable hospitality business and decided to resign from Thomas Financial. History repeated itself fifteen years after, when his father had resigned from

Reynolds to look after the business at the Winkler. Mit asked my advice on what to name the new company that would manage the new developments. My father taught me through his actions that one must always do the right thing, not always the easiest or most lucrative thing. Pappa inspired me that to have a genuine and noble heart is the greatest reflection of a man's character. Noble Investment Group was formed in October of 1994.

Shah Guys - Noble Investment Group

My friends Dr. Pankaj Vyas and Dr. Gulab Shah had shown interest in investing some of their funds with Noble. We invited them to join us. Mit and I went on the road to present investment opportunities with Noble, and we were successful in raising capital. Raj brought in investors from his circle of friends, including Jerome Bettis, then, the all-pro running back for the Pittsburgh Steelers.

In late 1994, Noble leased its first office space in Atlanta at Lenox Plaza on Peachtree Road in Buckhead. The space was one hundred square feet, with one desk and two chairs. Mit handled the business from there. I used the second chair when I visited Atlanta from Winston-Salem. In 1995, Noble's corporate office moved to the Atlanta Financial Center in Buckhead and occupied five thousand square feet of office space. The corporate accounting and operations staff increased. Mit got married in April 1995, and within a year, his father-in-law, Dr. Mahendra Patel, and some of his doctor friends joined Noble as investors. The infusion of funds gave another boost to Noble's growth. Noble had grown to twelve properties within five years of its inception. Each property had some of the same partners at various levels, all within my and Mahendra's friend circles. Mit decided to roll-up all the properties under one real estate fund entity and assign proportionate partnerships to all our friends. Noble first real estate fund was formed in 1999. As a surprise gesture, I named Mit Noble's president at the investors' conference in Jacksonville, Florida. The assets in Noble's first fund were sold during 2005 through 2007 with all the partners receiving a substantial return on their investments. In 2003, Noble was approached by private equity funds managers to invest in the hospitality sector. Mit took advantage of this new relationship and created even larger growth prospects for the organization with Noble's second real estate fund.

While Mit was focused in growing Noble, Raj attended the University of North Carolina at Chapel Hill for his undergraduate degree in business and finance. He went on to Cornell University and completed his master's degree in hospitality management. Raj joined Noble during mid-2001. He became vice president of acquisitions. The effects of September 11, 2001, were devastating to the hotel business. Hotel occupancy all through the country took a nose dive, and Noble was no exception. The money to acquire new properties dried up. Instead, the challenge was to survive through hard times, just making ends meet. It was a tough period for Mit. I saw him struggling through cash flow shortages and having to make difficult decisions. I helped him to stay focused, a lesson I had learned through four recessions that I had gone through. Raj, however, was using his network of relationships he developed at UNC and at Cornell to source distressed real estate opportunities in the depressed economy. In 2003, Raj formed Pinnacle Real Estate Fund to invest in shopping centers and office complexes. While at Cornell,

Raj had interned with Choice and Marriott Hotels at company headquarters. His performance had attracted the attention at the executive level. However, somehow they knew that this kid was destined to be in his own business. Raj has expanded Pinnacle Real Estate enterprise and has not only survived the recent recession but has maintained great profitability of the business at hand and is looking for more acquisitions.

Westin Hotel

I have to confess that Mit is a better manager than I ever was. He is a taskmaster, whereas I was lenient in demanding results. He was eager and took time to learn from great industry leaders their formula for success and growth and brought those philosophies to Noble. The company would not have made such a significant progress in the hospitality industry if Mit's talents were not involved in the financing, development, and management processes needed to strategically guide the growth of the organization. By 2006, Mit had brought in several of the best executives in the hospitality industry and made them partners at Noble. In 2007, Noble raised its third real estate fund with $310 million of equity committed by some of the most prominent public pension funds and university endowments in the United States. With a powerhouse team of leaders, Noble continued to develop significant in-house core competencies for investment management, project development and operations. In 2013, Noble reached the $2 billion mark in hotels it has invested in, half of which it has sold, and its portfolio on average achieves more than $1 million a day in revenue. As we drive by one of Noble's W Hotels, Milan often reminds me of the pride she feels when she looks at where we started with the "W" in Winkler and how Noble has progressed. It took thirty years of productive work by the old and young of the family, persevering through hard times, with honesty at each level of endeavor. Only in this country.

W Hotel

Hyatt Hotel

Mit and I used to attend major hospitality investment conferences as guests. Today, Mit is a sought-after speaker at those conferences. In one of the first times I saw him speak, Mit received the Hotelier of the Year award at the AAHOA convention in 2004. In his acceptance speech, Mit expressed his gratitude not only to his parents but to all those parents who had afforded such opportunity to their children, so open heartedly, to enter the hospitality industry. As tears rolled from my and Milan's eyes, I saw other parents wiping theirs, too. Mit repeats the sentiments whenever he makes a major speech.

In 2005, Noble acquired the two most prominent hotels in the city of Winston-Salem and negotiated the rights to manage the city-owned Benton Convention Center. Twenty-five years ago, Milan and I owned the Winkler, a mom-and-pop motel, located about a mile from these first-class properties. One hotel was a built as a Hyatt, and the other one was developed as a Stouffer's. Back then, Milan and I would sheepishly come downtown to see how these behemoths were run and what the clientele was like. We were wowed by the large ballrooms and the chandeliers that lighted the entire place. We were sure we could not dream of owning such a place, ever! Mit brought his parents back to these properties as nothing less than owners. Noble converted one of the hotels to an Embassy Suites and the other one to a full-service Marriott with a steakhouse known as WS Prime.

Marriott Hotel

Soon after the acquisition and conversion, Raj and I were in Winston-Salem and stayed at the Marriott. We met in the lobby that evening and started walking toward WS Prime for dinner. As we made our way into the restaurant, I saw about ten employees, including the head chef, standing in a line. They wanted to meet the chairman of company that delivered this great new hotel. I shook hands with every one of them, thanking them for their service to Noble and its guests. In return they thanked me for giving them an opportunity to work at the new Marriott. As I took my seat at the dining table, I prayed in gratitude on behalf of my family and the team members who worked for Noble. What a turnaround of events in thirty years. What a blessing.

Marriott Corporation has a tradition of recognizing hotel owners in their system every year. The owners' conference for the year 2007 was held in Barcelona, Spain. Mit arranged in a hurry for Milan and me to be in Barcelona just a week before the start of the conference. It was a three-day affair. At the gala dinner on the last evening, the annual awards were to be presented. Milan and I were assigned seats near the stage. At about the third announcement, Mit and Noble was presented with Marriott's Partnership Circle Award for Marriott's best partner. We were asked to join Mit and Mr. Bill Marriott, president and CEO of Marriott International, on the stage. Joy sparkled in my eyes.

The success within the hospitality industry is measured by the return on investment in cash. Children's expression of gratitude is the highest form of return that any parents would love to have. Milan and I have been fortunate to receive it in abundance. Friends and well-wishers ask me if I knew what the family business would become when I bought the Winkler thirty-three years ago. Not in my wildest dreams. I have a vivid memory of working on a room maintenance list with a toolbox in my left hand and a plunger in my right. The other memory is of giving finance lessons to Mit and Raj, at their young age, to develop five years' pro forma statements of hotel profitability. Many of my friends in hospitality industry have asked me how my humble beginnings led Noble to be such a powerhouse in the industry. I believe the early teaching of entrepreneurship, with the freedom to make their own decisions, provided the foundation for personal and professional growth for both Mit and Raj. The other important factor I had learned was that children must be given a proper education. When they show an interest in joining the family business, the parents should welcome it. As soon as it becomes evident that the kid has energy, knowledge of running the business with better tools, and the wherewithal of how to grow the bottom line, in general as evidence of business sense, parents should progressively start taking the backseat and let the next generation take over the business. Parents would then remain the guiding lights. I remind both Mit and Raj that we are blessed to have children like them; they tell us that they are doubly blessed to have parents like Milan and me.

CHAPTER 21
Personal Indulgences

When Jim Myers offered me the opportunity to buy the Winkler, he told me that I would make money. He had me promise him that I would pay him first to take care of the shortfall in my down payment. He also asked me that I would not go around buying new cars or create an extravagant lifestyle. He had me raise my right hand—and I had said, "Yes, I do!" In the next two years, I had not only fulfilled my promise to Jim Myers but had paid back all the money I borrowed from friends. Personally and deep down internally, I felt very good that at last, I was a free man financially.

As Milan kept looking for more and more investments, I kind of followed her lead, making sure that the investment made sense and that we did not have to borrow any money to make the deal. From my point of view, the time had come to enjoy life and fulfill some of the desires I'd had for so long and ignored in favor of developing my professional and family life.

Piedmont Aviation in Winston-Salem gave flying lessons. I called their office one day from Winkler and talked to a female instructor, who said she would call me back with a schedule. I briefly left the office to go to a bank. In my absence, Milan took the phone call from the instructor. The lady told Milan she had a schedule for me. Milan asked what the schedule was for. When she replied it was for flying lessons, my very smart wife replied, without any hesitation, "Oh, flying lessons? He decided not to take them." When I returned back from the bank, I was informed of the decision. Matter closed.

August 18, 1969, was the day of our first anniversary. I was a research scientist at Nabisco in Fairlawn, New Jersey. Mit had been born only eight days before. Returning home from work, I was actually rushing home to see Mit. All of a sudden it dawned on me that I had missed Milan's birthday, which was a day earlier; and today was our first anniversary, and I was about to miss that, too! I had rushed to a jewelry shop and had bought a one-carat diamond ring for an anniversary gift. I had paid one hundred dollars for it; a large sum, unaccounted for in my budget. The diamond color started getting gray within a month and went black within six months. When I took the ring back to the jewelry shop, the saleslady told me that that was the life of a Diamonair. I asked her to repeat the statement. She did. I said, "Why are you saying 'diamon air'? What is a diamon air?" Very calmly she explained that for a hundred dollars, I could only get a Diamonair, an artificial diamond. It would cost at least five thousand dollars for a one-carat ring. Five thousand dollars! That amounted to half a year of my salary at Nabisco. I brought the ring home, and Milan just kept it in a box with other pieces of her jewelry.

August 1982 was a different period. Now was the time to study real diamonds. I wanted to get even for the Diamonair! Carol Conrad, my desk superstar at the Winkler, knew a few things about diamonds. Her father, besides being a high school principal, was a certified gemologist. I called up Mr. Conrad and got the scoop on diamonds and decided not to get cheated anymore. He advised me to take lessons at Gemological Institute of America (GIA) on Forty-Seventh Street in New York City. He helped me to get registered, and soon I was on my way to New York. For the next seven days, I studied hundreds of diamonds under a microscope. Then, for the following week, I analyzed each diamond with a tong and a loop, a jeweler's standard equipment, for color, clarity, and carat size, the three "Cs" of diamond grading. I was very good at it, to the point I could pretty well grade a diamond with the naked eye. At the end of my course, I asked Milan to fly to New York with the precious first-anniversary gray diamond ring. With help from Mr. Conrad, we fitted the setting with a real one-carat, top-quality diamond. Even today, I am pretty good at grading a diamond, even if it is set in jewelry. Once again both Milan and I were happy for making a final correction, albeit thirteen years later!

During the 1970s, work at RJR was not taxing. I had plenty of free time to spend with my family and to develop some hobbies. Forsyth Technical Institute was my favorite place for taking weekend classes. I had completed small engine repairs very successfully. I was a favorite student of my teacher. Budd Crepps was a friend from RJR, and we used to spend a lot of time working on car engines. Both of us decided to take an auto painting class at Forsyth Tech. After completing the course, we thought we were good, and we decided to paint one of our cars. I had a Plymouth Duster with a metallic silver color. I had bought it in 1971 when I worked at Nabisco. By 1977, it needed a paint job. Budd and I prepared a shed next to his garage and started working on the Duster. We sanded the original paint down, primed it, and spray-painted it. It took two weeks of evening work, but the final product looked like a brand new car. A few months later, the paint started chipping in globs, and the red primer started showing through. The car looked like a zebra with red and silver dots. I still had the same car when we bought Winkler in 1979, and I still had it till 1982. That was the car I drove around town. Now the time had come to let it go.

One afternoon, after making a bank deposit, I decided to swing by a Mercedes Benz dealership in town. I had reviewed the prices on the new models and was prepared to talk. As I pulled into the dealership parking lot, a salesperson who was standing at the entrance door saw me coming out of the Duster. As I approached him, he asked if he could be of any help.

I told him I wanted to buy a Mercedes Benz.

He replied, "Doesn't everyone?"

I knew what he meant by that statement. I asked him to please show me what was available and tell me their cost.

He said, "Sir, they're all expensive."

I said, "I know."

He took me toward the used car lot and started showing me some cars, quoting prices for each. I kind of stopped him and asked him to show me the new ones in the showroom.

He stopped and turned to me. "Sir, I just want to let you know that they are very expensive."

I answered again, "I know."

The conversation was repeated a few times. Finally, I decided to go for a 300 D, Turbo Diesel that was priced at $32,000. My color of choice was beige.

The salesman asked, "And, sir, how do you intend to pay for the car?"

I answered, "Cash."

He just about hit the floor. He recovered himself and murmured, "Yes, of course, of course!" and jumped on the computer to locate the car from the dealership pool.

After about two days, the car arrived from Danville, Virginia. Milan and I went to pick it up with a cashier's check in hand. My dream of owning a brand new Mercedes Benz was fulfilled. Even after going through many Mercedes-Benz cars, I still have my 300D jewel, with its odometer sitting at nearly 250,000 miles.

Mercedes Benz - 1982

The K&W cafeteria in Winston-Salem is our favorite place for lunch. On one visit during 2005, Milan and I picked up our food selections and were taking our seats at a table. As I was sitting down, I saw a person staring at me. As I started eating, I kind of glanced at him and saw him still looking at me. I finally got up and went over to him. "Sir, I am Bart Shah. Do I know you from somewhere?"

He said, "Mr. Shah, I sold you your first Mercedes Benz." Happily, we shook hands. What a surprise! The man recognized me, even after twenty-three years of making the deal! And here is the beauty: We had sold Winkler in 1996. The salesperson told me that he sold the new owner of Winkler his first Mercedes Benz, too. How lovely!

By 1984, we had been at the Loch Drive house for about ten years. The Town and Country subdivision was considered about the third-best community in the city. Buena Vista was where the town's elite lived, and that's where the Shah family wanted to move to. The top real estate broker in town was Emma Graham of Graham and Boles Real Estate. We asked Emma to help us find a home in Buena Vista. We looked at many estate homes in Buena Vista. All of them were large, with white columns in the front. The interiors were beautifully done; the backyards had ornate gardens. Milan just loved one house. It was so palatial that it really would have been the ideal address, but Bharat, the flavor chemist with a million-dollar nose, smelled mildew in the basement of all the houses we looked at. Besides, the houses in Buena Vista were traditional homes. We, with our Indian taste, were looking for a contemporary home, and there were none available in Buena Vista. We decided to build our dream home from ground up. As Emma began looking for a lot, she called Bill Adams, a homebuilder who specialized in custom-built contemporary homes, to find out if he was doing any spec homes we could look at. Bill mentioned a lot that could be available because the present owner had asked him to stop work on the already planned home on the lot. Emma called the owner to find out if the lot was for sale. He was furious, wanting to know how she could possibly know about his personal plans. His answer was short: "The lot is not for sale."

Two weeks later Emma got a call from the owner of the lot, and instead of pricing the lot himself, he asked her to bring an offer. At that stage Emma contacted us and told us about the lot—but the lot was about twenty minutes outside the city. I asked if it was so spectacular that it was worth the commute into town every day. She said, "I know it is." We soon took a drive, and lo and behold, we were entering the Bermuda Run Country Club. The last time I had entered those gates was in 1972, at the RJR Christmas party. The lot belonged to Billy Satterfield, the eccentric developer of Bermuda Run Country Club. This was the best lot in the entire development, and he had retained it for himself. What a beautiful view—a golf course with the thirteenth green and fourteenth tee as a backyard, surrounded by lakes and willow trees! The front had a lily pond with a lighted fountain. Milan and I were totally enchanted by the most beautiful location for a home we had ever seen in our lives. That evening we wrote up an offer, and Emma presented it to Mr. Satterfield. After a few back-and-forth negotiations, in the summer of 1984, we bought the land in an all-cash transaction.

Bharat & Milan

Twelve years earlier I had entered the gates of Bermuda Run Country Club. I had rehearsed the driving direction three times just to make sure that I arrived on time for my first Christmas party. I was uneasy to begin with, but then a welcome salute from a white officer at the gate to young Indian man made me realize that I was at a special place. When I saw the development then, I wondered who would live in such an elite place, what kind of business or professions would someone be in to afford to live in there? Well, soon enough it was the Shah family's address, with the most beautiful vista in Bermuda Run Country Club.

Milan and I would visit Atlanta every month after Noble's office was opened in 1994. We really did not think of moving to Atlanta for business reasons. The arrival of our first grandchild, Arjun, in February 1998 was the primary reason for our move to Atlanta in 1999. As we looked for a permanent residence, Sugarloaf Golf and Country Club was our choice. After looking at many homes, we decided to build a small one for ourselves. As we went through the details of our desired floor plan, the builder brought us to a spec house under construction at 2877 Darlington Run, to show us its floor plan. If we liked the plan, he intended to duplicate it on a smaller footprint. The house was too big for the two of us. However, the floor plan and the view of a beautiful lake in the backyard got us hooked. That is where Milan and I now live—one of the best locations in Sugarloaf Country Club.

Sugarloaf Home

Bharat & Milan - Sugarloaf Home Backyard

During my childhood in Navapur, I was a member of a struggling middle-class family. My college years in India didn't show me a better future path, either. Master's and doctorate degrees in the United States only brought a career that allowed us to scrape by financially. It was at the age of forty that life took a turn for the better with the opportunity to buy the Winkler Motor Inn. This was the time to enjoy life and the financial freedom we had achieved. These personal indulgences were not spectacular by any means, but they meant a great deal for me, considering where my life's journey had begun.

CHAPTER 22
The Asian American Hotel Owners Association

Many Indian immigrants all around the country had entered the hospitality business by mid-1980. Most of us had bought old, rundown mom-and-pop independent motels. Basically, we had bought the right to provide our own labor and hoped to make a living. The properties we bought were, in most cases, old and required a lot of repairs. Husband and wife and sometimes grown up children had to work in cleaning the linen, making rooms, handling repairs and managing the front desk. Some, with good luck and foresight, had progressed to be owners of franchised properties like Comfort Inn, Days Inn, and Econo Lodge, all of which were in the economy segment of the hospitality industry.

In 1985 Mike Leven became the new president of the hotel franchise company Days Inns of America. Running a franchise company was new to Mike. After moving to the company headquarters in Atlanta, Mike wanted to know all about how the company was managed, who the customers were, the process for the revenue stream, and the expense structure. He invited senior executives to his office to brief him. He did understand the guts of a franchise company and the importance of a relationship with the franchisees—their customers. He was told that Days Inns had a good base of American franchisees, and lately some Indians had also been given the franchise rights. Mike was told not to be concerned with a small group of Indians, because they were basically categorized as "Curry Palaces." Every Indian-owned motel had the smell of curry in its lobby because the family living quarters would be right behind the front desk.

Mike was amused by the term "Curry Palaces" but understood the implications. He had learned that there were only two criteria by which to rate franchisees: the quality rating of the operation and whether the franchise fees were being paid on time or not. He asked for a summary report on the franchisees before making a judgment one way or the other. The report showed that as for quality ratings, the Indian owners were on par with other franchisees in the system, but the Indians were ahead in timeliness in paying their dues. Mike knew the Indians were being discriminated against within his own company. He believed that something had to be done to make the group aware of discrimination and get them unified to confront it wherever it was happening in the hospitality industry. Mike invited a few of the Indian franchisees of Days Inn to come visit him in Atlanta. Among them were H. P. Rama of Greenville, South Carolina, and Harish Pattni and Nitin Shah of Atlanta. Mike gave them a status report of what was happening to the Indian franchisees of Days Inn of America, explaining it was probably the same in any other hotel franchise company as well. He offered his personal help as well as that of Days Inns of America. He invited every Indian in the hospitality business to come to Atlanta for a one-day conference. He wished to give all the Indian owners an opportunity to get to know each other and to explain to them the need for a unified front.

It was summer of 1986 when I received a letter of invitation for a hospitality conference in Atlanta. Milan and I drove from Winston-Salem and checked in at the Days Inn in downtown Atlanta. There were about a hundred attendees at the conference, mainly from the Southeast. The day's activities were mainly learning the business, meeting other attendees, and hearing Mike Leven's message for us about forming an association. This was music to my ears. Just four years earlier, Governor Jim Hunt had the same message for us in North Carolina. India Merchants Association was his brainchild, and we had already experienced the benefits of being united. Mike's appeal for a national organization attracted me. During the next three years, many active Indian hoteliers, under the guidance of Mike Leven, worked out the formation, constitution, and bylaws of the new association. It was named Asian American Hotel Owners Association (AAHOA). The first meeting was held in 1989 with Days Inn of America footing the $100,000 bill. About 350 of us came together this time in downtown Atlanta. Some well-known, successful Indian immigrants, representing various industries, gave presentations about their various paths to success. All the speakers had the same underlying message: the United States of America was the land of opportunity if we worked hard and were honest in our personal and professional dealings. One of the speakers was H. P. Rama, who was very instrumental in bringing the thought of an association to fruition. H. P.'s company, JHM Hotels probably had the largest hotel portfolio in the group at that time. I liked H. P.'s oratory style and demeanor onstage. He compared himself to Arjun of the Hindu scripture Geeta, and Mike Leven to Lord Krishna, who drove Arjun's chariot in the war against evil forces. H. P. was chosen to be the founding chairman of AAHOA.

I had decided to run for a seat as a board member at large. The next AAHOA convention was held in 1992 in Nashville, Tennessee. My friends from North Carolina and Mohanbhai and his friends from Florida did all the canvassing for me, covering the entire country. I gave a two-minute speech onstage to let the audience know who I was and why I was qualified for the position and their votes. Other candidates did the same. When the votes were counted, I had the highest number of votes, and my entire circle of friends from North Carolina were excited. Mohanbhai knew that I would do well. Nitin Shah, who had been on the board ever since the inception of the association, was an election official who counted the votes. As I came off the stage, thanking the members for their confidence in me, Nitin met me at the bottom of the steps and friendly cursed me in typical Gujarati, saying, "Who the hell are you?" He was smiling when he said it, happy to see another hotel owner with a similar last name who was also interested in community work through AAHOA.

Bharat at Community Event

Ravi Patel of Charlotte, North Carolina, was elected the 1992 chairman of AAHOA. I knew Ravi because he was instrumental in building the Hindu Center in Charlotte, where I was a life member. Later on during the year, Ravi asked me to become a convention chairman for the year-end annual gathering. Orlando, Florida, was selected as the convention city, as we wanted to attract potential members from Florida. The three-day convention was a super hit. Milan had selected various menus for each meal and made sure the breakfast included Indian masala tea. She was in the kitchen at five each morning to guide meal preparations for the entire day. The attendance of 850 people was beyond our expectations, and everybody enjoyed the educational seminars and AAHOA hospitality.

Nitin Shah was elected as 1993 Chairman of AAHOA. Harish Pattni was elected Vice Chairman. The year 1993 was probably the most active and productive, with significant membership growth. The Nitin-Harish team had almost forty-five meetings and regional conferences all around the country. The association membership reached almost 3000 that year. As Vice Chair for the year 1993, Harish Pattni was in line to be the

Chairman in 1994. Having been a board member in 1992 and a convention chairman for 1993, I was ready to move up to the Vice Chairman's position. I had learned the ins and outs of the association and had a good relationship with many industry leaders. Far before the 1993 convention, I had started making phone calls to all the board members of my decision to run for the Vice Chairman's position. I called Nitin, and he was very supportive of the plan. Nitin was a very close friend of J. K. Patel, one of the board members. J. K. had also thought of running for the Vice Chairman's position. When J. K. found out that I was making phone calls to cover my base, one night he called me. In a very gracious overture, he told me that he would support me that year and asked me to support him the next year. I happily accepted his request and thanked him for being so generous.

At the annual convention, Harish was confirmed as 1994 Chairman. I won the election unanimously and became Vice Chairman. As Harish and I traveled together, we came to know each other well and started working as a team. Harish liked my attention to detail and getting things done on time. Together we conducted about thirty-five meetings and regional conferences. The 1994 convention was to be held at the Opryland Hotel in Nashville, Tennessee. The number of attendees at the previous convention was about 1,200. The plan was made to accommodate around 1,400 to 1,500 for this convention. During the year, Harish was in negotiations to bring Indian movie superstar and an idol Amitabh Bachchan as a keynote speaker for the 1994 convention. When it was confirmed, all the board members were notified of the new development. The news flashed all over the country in Indian news media. AAHOA took out advertisements in some prominent Indian newspapers to inform the members of the new development.

On December 10, 1994, the day the convention opened at Opryland, all hell broke loose. A total of 4,200 people stood as an unruly crowd for registration. It was difficult to convince them to form lines. We made new arrangements for meeting venues, invited Indian chefs from all around the country at any price, and asked them to bring Indian groceries with them, as all Nashville stores had gone empty. Harish pleaded with the crowd to cooperate, and finally they did. The AAHOA convention of 1994 brought the association to the forefront of the industry associations.

Vendors recognized the strength of AAHOA members because the value of goods sold at that convention broke all past records.

Amitabh Bachchan arrived at 5a.m., straight from Bombay. As he came onstage, the crowd went wild. They had never, for the life of them, ever thought they would see this iconic star in person. Amitabh offered good wishes for the two associations, AAHOA and IAHI (Indo-American Hospitality Association), coming together during the convention. His message was congratulatory and upbeat. Amitabh was a lead actor in the movie "Agni Path", Path of Fire. The movie depicted a human's life as if going through a forest burning with fire. The message was that one should not expect a protection of a shadow even from a small leaf of a tree. He challenged us not to seek any help or pity from anyone while going through this difficult stage in an enterprise of our choice, the hospitality industry. Amitabh's profound message made a great impact on the invited guests from the industry. Upon requests from the audience, he recited some famous dialogs from his movies. The audience cheered him wildly. After the hectic beginning with an unexpected crowd in attendance, the first day's morning session set the stage for a memorable convention in AAHOA's history.

On the last day of the convention, I was elected the Chairman for 1995. As promised, I had arranged for J. K. Patel to be nominated as Vice Chairman, and he was elected unanimously. Shankarbhai Patel of Nashville, Tennessee, and his team of board members from IAHI were my ardent supporters. Harish introduced me as the new AAHOA Chairman during the evening gala dinner. I started my acceptance speech by thanking Mike Leven, a visionary for bringing us together. Then I moved on to a very motivational theme and my goals for the coming year. I could feel the excitement in the air from the audience's enthusiastic response. I knew I had done well the first day on the job.

Bharat & Milan

CHAPTER 23
AAHOA Chairman, 1995

At this point in time, my responsibility and commitment was to AAHOA and the community it served. Milan stepped up to manage the family-owned properties in my absence. Whenever I was in town, I tried to hire a manager, train the person to some degree, and return to Atlanta. We ended up going through four different managers that year, with a significant revenue loss at Winkler.

The first order of business was to put in place systems and processes at the AAHOA office to ensure the association could be efficient and sustainable for future growth. In my opinion, there were several staff members that had let Harish down with their work habits. I kept only a couple of staff members who were in charge of membership data. I needed them to help me with upgrading the system. I figured we had about $540,000 in cash and CDs as I reviewed the bank statements. The bills from Opryland and other convention vendors were piling up. They were for large amounts, as the convention attendance was more than 3,000 over our planned budget for 1,500 attendees. I spent the next two weeks negotiating with Opryland to give us some relief. At the end, when all the outstanding invoices were paid, AAHOA's treasury was left with $40,000. I sat down with all the numbers and made an analysis of convention revenue and expenses. The total cost of a three-day convention came down to $250 per attendee. The registration fee was $100 per attendee - meaning that AAHOA lost $150 per attendee. I prepared my presentation for the first board meeting in Atlanta. My report was shocking for how much we had lost and why. The board immediately approved raising the next year's convention fees to $250 per attendee.

The two staff members who handled data management could not work under the strict new guidelines. One day, when I arrived at the office from Winston-Salem, both of them had cleared their desks and gone! Except for the chairman, the AAHOA office had no supporting staff whatsoever. I needed someone whom I could trust to get things moving the way I wanted to. One year is a very short time for a chairman to accomplish anything constructive, especially in the environment I was in. Our friend Mohanbhai's younger daughter, Harshna, who lived in metro Atlanta, had an MBA degree in accounting. I talked to Harshna, and she was happy to join. I put her in charge of AAHOA accounting, receivables from franchisors, allied members, and regular membership dues. Being a Gujarati, well versed in computer technology and with an accounting background, Harshna cleaned up duplications in membership data and provided an actual status of AAHOA finances. Priti Patel who was referred by Shankarbhai to apply for a job, was AAHOA's second employee. I moved AAHOA office to Buckhead, Atlanta's financial district. Milan contacted some hotel furniture companies to donate furniture for the new office and got it well furnished. Very soon thereafter we hired Rachael Williams as the new executive director and had her hire the support staff she needed. I kept the budget tight. Later on, with Harshna and Priti's help, we developed AAHOA's budget for 1995.

AAHOA Chairman - 1995

I had developed a good relationship with board members all around the nation.

J. K., the Vice Chairman; J. P. Rama, who was a Treasurer; Jay Patel from Colorado; Raxit Shah from Ohio; Pravin Khatiwala from New Jersey; and Ketan Masters from Texas became the members of my inner circle. Many of us traveled together to conduct regional conferences around the country. In my speeches I carried the theme of "Walking through a Burning Forest" that I had picked up from Amitabh Bachchan's message at the 1994 AAHOA convention. The most motivational theme came from a water fountain story that actually belonged to a good friend of mine, Ashvin Shah from Spartanburg, South Carolina. Ashvin and his friend, both engineers, landed at the JFK airport in New York when they arrived for the first time as students from India. As they got off the plane, they were thirsty and were looking for a public water stand, a standard in India. Upon inquiring, they were directed toward a water fountain. There were no such facilities in India during the 1960s, and the engineers could not figure out how to get water from the stainless steel box. When a little girl arrived, she pushed a button on the side, and water flew from a small opening. She had to bend down to sip the water. Picking up on that, my message to the members of AAHOA was that the hospitality business was our secret button in quenching our thirst for financial independence. However, we have to bend down, work hard, remain humble and show humility while we quench our thirst, the thirst for financial freedom! Even today, almost twenty years later, I get reminded of that profound life message by many of the members and vendors whenever I am at an AAHOA event.

AAHOA Board - 1995

When I was vice chairman, Tarun Kapoor, a professor at Pomona Technical Institute in Pomona, California, had asked me for my vision of initiating education programs for AAHOA members during my year as chairman. Having been a single-property owner and then growing into the ownership of a few others, I had discovered a gap in my experience in managing more than one property at a time. I was spending most of my time putting out fires instead of creating strategic planning for future growth. I told Tarun I wanted to initiate an educational program for AAHOA members to learn multiproperty management. Tarun promised he would develop such a program and present it to us before the end of the year. I liked the plan when he presented it in January 1995. I invited Tarun to present to the board. We all liked it. The Institute of Business Management was formed at AAHOA to undertake educational programs. Later on the name was changed to AAHOA Institute of Management. As the theme of multiproperty management spread through the country, and members all over had a positive experience, the seminar became the main focus of all regional conferences. Ever since then, Tarun Kapoor has been associated with AAHOA, providing many seminars covering various disciplines related to the hospitality industry and being a moderator for AAHOA's strategic planning process year after year.

San Francisco, California, is the birthplace of the Indian hospitality industry in the United States. I attended every regional conference in California from the time I came aboard in 1992. For some reason, the local attendance was very small, and even with increased publicity, the numbers did not change. During my year as vice chairman, a few youngsters who represented third-generation hoteliers in San Francisco—Mike Amin, Pramod Patel, and Mahendra Patel—asked me to let them coordinate the California conference in 1995 when I would be AAHOA chairman. During February 1995, Mike Amin called me at the AAHOA office to line up a date for a conference in San Francisco. We set a date for July. The group of AAHOA board members arrived in San Francisco the night before the conference. We had dinner with the organizers and were told that the next day's conference would be better than the one last year. I expected a crowd of about eighty to one hundred people. The next morning when I came down to the ballroom area from my room, I could not believe my eyes. There was a large crowd of almost seven hundred attendees. They were being welcomed by about thirty young ladies, all clad in white saris, greeting the guests in the Indian hand-clasped prayer style.

They were catching everyone who walked in and asking if he or she was a member. They recruited a large number of members with payment on the spot. We had invited the "pioneers," the first-generation Indian hoteliers, and recognized them at the conference. The atmosphere was lively and even better than the AAHOA annual convention. I was very impressed with the work the group had done and came to respect the capability of the young hoteliers. The California conference was one of the very best in 1995.

As I was walking in the hotel lobby while attending the California conference, a gentleman approached me and told me that my face was very familiar and that he knew me from somewhere. I went as far back as 1970 when I worked for Nabisco and lived in Parsippany, New Jersey. He had never been to any of the towns I mentioned. Then he asked me where I went to school in the United States. When I answered Knoxville, Tennessee, he jumped in joy. He said, "Oh, you are Bhidu", the Dear Friend! I asked him for his name. He said he was Gopal Bhakta. Gopal was the senior most of the Gujarati students who lived in one house and had their meals together. I was the "grocery delivery man" with my 1954 Pontiac. Bhakta and I were meeting again after thirty years, and he still had fond memories of our friendship.

As the program continued on the stage, I finished with a very up-beat motivational speech before the gala dinner. As I came off the stage, Mike Amin and his friends, jubilant for the success of the conference, came to see me. They had a few of the successful hoteliers with them and wanted me to meet them. I shook hands with everyone and thanked them for their support. One of them, a man with a big potbelly, was introduced to me as a top gun of San Francisco. His name was R. M. Patel. He told me that there was a young man by the last name of Shah whom he knew when he was a student at Wilson College in Bombay. He did not remember his name. I asked him what year he was at Wilson. He said 1956 to 1958. I asked him what his major was. He replied that it was math. Then I asked him what the initials R. M. stood for. He said Raman Madhav. I scolded him, saying, "*Kaka* (Uncle), you had such a skinny body with a twenty-eight-inch waist. What have you done to yourself with this big belly?"

As soon as he heard being addressed as "Kaka," his eyes sparkled. He said, "Oh my God, you are my *dikro*, my son!" He told me that he was sitting at the back, and when he heard my voice from the podium, he felt that he had heard the voice somewhere before. It was at Mackichan Hall, the Wilson College dormitory, as I stood on the stage delivering my annual speech as a general secretary, almost forty years earlier. Raman was a couple of years ahead of me at Wilson College and was our advisor for any problem our group of friends had, educational or personal. We lovingly called him Uncle, *Kaka*.

One of the most active board members on my team was Ketan Masters from Dallas, Texas. We conducted a tri-city—Dallas, Houston, and San Antonio—regional conference in those cities in three days. A.V. Patel of Dallas and Hasu Patel of Houston provided great organizational help. I was at the podium in Dallas, and many from the audience asked for the 1995 annual convention to be in Dallas. During all the past years, the annual convention was held along the East Coast, just because there were more members in the region. For the first time ever, I would bring the convention west. In return, I asked for enthusiastic cooperation from the community. Dallas community leaders jumped on the stage and declared their full cooperation. We announced the decision during the next few days at Houston and San Antonio. The state of Texas was ecstatic. In lining up the local support for the convention, J. K., J. P., and I made several trips to Dallas thereafter. We stayed at Ketan's house, nicknamed Ketanashram, Ketan's Hermitage. Chan and Surekha Patel were the most respected couple in the community, and they still are today. They were my choice as the hosts for the Dallas convention and were asked to receive dignitaries at Dallas airport.

During one of the earlier trips to Dallas, I had met Jags Patel, one of the best information technology experts in the region. I invited Jags to come to Atlanta because AAHOA membership data needed to be updated and fine-tuned. Jags made many visits to the Atlanta office and worked with Harshna. Jags was my choice to handle the convention registration process. I also met a gentleman named Vinod Patel, who was a lead coordinator for food services to the large Indian community in Dallas. I approached Vinod and asked him for his help during the convention. He was excited and agreed. I felt so good about the enthusiastic reception that I called Dallas my hometown thereafter.

Jay Patel from Colorado Springs was another very active board member. Jay was an accomplished musician and played many instruments. He was my choice for controlling audio/video presentations during the convention. Pravin Khatiwala, known as the King of Atlantic City, New Jersey, was a regional director from the state. The Edison Conference was one of the largest we ever had in that area. All these large, well-attended conferences added a lot of new members to AAHOA. The membership had reached close to four thousand members by the end of 1995.

Joe McInerny, the past president of American Hotel and Lodging Association (AH&LA), was then the president and CEO of the Travelodge franchise company. Greg Plank was a senior vice president. Joe and Greg had tremendous respect for the young association of AAHOA, and Travelodge was a major sponsor of AAHOA educational seminars. I maintained good personal relationships with the franchise company executives. Instead of badgering them on the AAHOA stage over the franchise issues, my mode of operation was to gather members' concerns and make sure they were honest. I would arrange for a meeting with the franchisor representatives. I would invite the board members, especially the ones whose members had complaints, to join me at the meeting. Don Landry was then the president of Choice Hotels International, the franchise company that represented the Econo Lodge and Comfort Inn brands. We reached Silver Springs, Maryland, the night before our meeting with the Choice Hotels executives. I apprised the board members of the issues we were going to discuss the next morning. In just one morning session with Don and his company representatives, we resolved many issues on the spot. The right people approach, rather than a confrontational one, has proven to be the business strategy that has worked best for me.

Curtis Nelson, then the executive vice president and COO of Carlson Hospitality Worldwide in Minneapolis, Minnesota, was a friend of AAHOA. The company had just established its new brand, Country Inn and Suites. The entire board was invited to Minneapolis for a dinner at the family estate. Marilyn Nelson, then the president of the company, spoke highly of AAHOA, its mission, and its accomplishments to date. The next morning we were introduced to the new brand and were escorted to lunch at the Executive Lounge. There, the founder, Mr. Curtis Carlson, Marilyn's father, handed me a check for $50,000 as the first installment toward AAHOA's educational efforts. He also promised part of a franchise fee, collected from AAHOA member franchisees, to go toward AAHOA's education programs. The commitment continues even today, almost eighteen years after that first generous gesture. Since then, many franchise companies have participated in scholarship projects for AAHOA.

It was time to start planning for the annual convention in Dallas. Ketan Masters had set up a meeting with the Hotel Anatole management to handle the final negotiations and planning. J. K., the vice chairman, most of the board members, and I reached Dallas the night before the meeting. I had in my hand a complete analysis of expenses related to every segment of the last year's convention. My message was that we would make every effort to save as much as possible in our negotiations, concentrating on major expense items that would make a larger impact. The next morning, we were at the negotiating table with the Anatole staff. I found Raxit Shah, who sat next to me, to be the best negotiator for the deal. At the end of the day, in total, we had saved $140,000 compared to the previous year's convention for similar services. The local crowd got word of our smashing success and came to the Dallas airport to celebrate the day with us. We had one of the largest and loudest beer parties ever!

The convention planning began in earnest in October. Jags Patel was ready with the registration process. Ranjan Surati, wife of a board member, Ramesh Surati, proposed to bring in a large contingent of volunteers, all young students from around the country. They were computer literate, bilingual, and willing to work hard to help with the registration process, giving directions to various events and helping to coordinate food lines. Jags and Ranjan made plans to bring the young volunteers for training a couple of days before the convention.

We had planned many events and processes that were being introduced for the first time in an AAHOA annual convention. A Tender Loving Care (TLC) room was established for handling any unresolved issues at the registration desk. All the board members were asked to be present near the registration area. As soon as a volunteer at a registration desk encountered a confrontational issue with a member, he/she would raise a hand. A board member would approach the counter and escort the member to a room specially manned to resolve issues. He or she would be served refreshments while the individual's registration was processed. The customer service and process helped to move the registration lines pleasantly and quickly.

A board members' appreciation dinner was planned for the first evening of the convention. This was a formal event, by invitation only, where only the board members and their immediate family members were honored for their sacrifice of time and money and their service to AAHOA during the year. Allied members and vendors were very important for AAHOA's progress. We invited them to a special room, provided an open bar and food service, and recognized their contribution to AAHOA. Another first in the convention planning process was to recognize the franchise company presidents at an event coined "Breakfast with the Presidents." Each attending President was partnered with a board member, who would escort the officer for every convention event. These events have remained part of the annual conventions ever since.

Bharat and JK with Mike Leven

I reached Dallas about three days before the convention. The board members, volunteers, and vendors were trickling in slowly. I had brought with me a small temple of Hindu gods and goddesses and had placed it in my room. Every morning I would pray "I took the responsibility of running the association for this year for no other reason but in a spirit of being a volunteer for community work. There was no personal ego involved in undertaking the task. As of today, I had done as much humanly possible to accomplish the assigned work. Now, as the final days are approaching, I leave it to you, Almighty, to guide me as I step outside this room."

I went to the registration floor on the first day. All who entered had their package in less than two minutes. There were no long lines. The members loved the TLC treatment. The Dallas Cowboys cheerleaders opened the 1995 convention. With loud music in the background, they entered the stage and stomped the floor. The audience went crazy. There had never been an AAHOA convention opening like this before! J. K. Patel, the vice chairman of AAHOA, invited me to give the opening speech. I enumerated the accomplishments of the year, which included initiation of the educational seminars, an increase in membership, and, most importantly, bringing stability to AAHOA's financial condition. We had instituted new approaches to achieve the goal and were leaving $860,000 in the AAHOA coffers.

Dev Anand, my favorite actor from Bollywood, was in the United States, as a guest of Dr. Ramesh Japra, publisher of *India Post*. Ramesh brought Dev Anand to the AAHOA convention. We were elated to have him. The next day, during the evening, Dev Anand charmed the audience, congratulating the hardworking AAHOA members for their achievement in the US hospitality industry.

Bharat with Mike Leven at AAHOA Convention - 1995

The gala night is traditionally reserved for AAHOA awards. I had invited Mike Leven, the founding father of AAHOA, to give out the awards to the recipients. I wanted to bestow the honor on Mike before leaving as the Chairman. Finally, I introduced J. K. Patel as our next Chairman. Milan and I made a final round to meet the friends who had made this evening—and, for that matter, the entire year of accomplishments—possible.

The hospitality media ranked the convention as one of the best in the industry. That evening, as I walked back to our room, my heart was satisfied that our team did a great job. When I reached our room, I bowed at the temple in sincere gratitude for all the divine help that had been given during the year for the accomplishments beyond my wildest dreams.

CHAPTER 24
Mit's Wedding

Milan and Manju Bhoola have remained close friends ever since they were roommates in college. Manju and her family lived in Johannesburg, South Africa. When Manju left for Johannesburg for good, she told Milan that after being married, if she had a daughter, she would name her Milan. Manju's first child was a girl, and, as promised, she named her Milan. The Bhoola family moved to Daytona Beach, Florida, during the late 1970s when young Milan was a teenager. After a few years, she arrived in Atlanta to attend Emory University. There she met a young man, Alpesh Patel. After a couple of years of dating, plans were made for Milan and Alpesh to be engaged. It was the summer of 1992.

My wife, Milan, and I reached Daytona Beach to attend the engagement ceremony. Young Milan had arrived with her group of friends. Out of all these girls, one stood out because of her beauty and poise—and she was the coordinator for the entire ceremony. That's quite a job for a young lady! I asked my wife, Milan, to find out the girl's name and whereabouts from Manju. Her name was Reshma Patel. Mit was in Atlanta, and I knew I had to give him this information! I called him and told him I had found a beautiful girl for him. He asked me what she looked like. I described what she looked like and told him she was a friend of Milan's from Emory. Mit just smiled and said that he had seen her at Manjumasi's house about three years back but could not remember her name. I told him that her name was Reshma Patel. Mit remembered that and said, "That's it, Reshma Patel." I told him to get to know her when she was back in Atlanta. Reshma was in medical school and with Mit being in Atlanta, he did not have a chance to meet her. Meanwhile, Mit had gotten in touch with young Milan and had the chance to meet her fiancé, Alpesh. In no time, Mit and Alpesh became the best of friends.

Alpesh and Milan's wedding was planned for June of 1993. My wife, Milan, and I were there. So were Alpesh and Milan's friends. Most of them had traveled by car from Atlanta. During the prewedding parties, I did not see any signs of a relationship developing between Mit and Reshma. I was disappointed that my son was all caught up in the groom's parties and wasn't even attempting to get to know Reshma. The morning after Alpesh and Milan's wedding, we returned to Atlanta.

Alpesh's friends raided the honeymoon suite by tricking the hotel desk clerks, claiming that they were from a decoration company. When Alpesh and Milan arrived in the suite, the gang had a special welcome for them. After a while, they left the newly married couple alone and had their own nightlong party.

The next morning the caravan was getting ready to leave for Atlanta. One of Mit's friends, Rajeev, who was a coordinator for the caravan, found Reshma in her car by herself. He went looking for someone to keep her company and found Mit sleeping in his friend Aman's car. He asked Mit to get up and join Reshma on the drive back to Atlanta. The caravan left, and on the way their conversation got so interesting that at a lunch break, Reshma and Mit sat at a separate table to continue their discussion. Their friends realized something was in the air. Unknown to us, the relationship was going to grow to a serious level!

Reshma was back in her hometown of Toccoa in North Georgia for a quick summer break. Mit had continued keeping in touch with Reshma and met her frequently. During August of 1993, Milan and I were in Los Angeles at my sister Saryu's house. We were on our way to take a cruise in Alaska to celebrate our twenty-fifth anniversary. Saryu knocked at our bedroom door and said there was a phone call from Mit. I looked at the clock; it was four in the morning! I was frightened and grabbed the phone. "Are you all right?" I exclaimed. Mit asked me to calm down and said he had some good news for us. He had not been able to sleep all night and had decided to call us at seven in the morning, Atlanta time, not thinking about the time difference. Mit had visited Reshma's parents and asked for their blessings before proposing to Reshma. He was going to propose to her later that day in Winston-Salem. That evening Mit put a ring on Reshma's finger at the Reynolda Gardens by Wake Forest University, in Mit's favorite neighborhood, the most beautiful flower garden in Winston-Salem.

After the Alaska cruise, we met Reshma's parents, Mahendra and Ranjan, at their home. We also met Reshma's two younger sisters, Tejal and Nirali, each one as pretty as Reshma. We found them all so friendly, as if the two families had a long-standing relationship. Mit and Reshma were engaged in May of 1994. The engagement ceremony was at our home in Bermuda Run in North Carolina. The ceremony and the evening reception were as beautiful and elaborate as a marriage ceremony. The only thing left out was for the two of them to exchange garlands, a tradition signifying wedding. It was an occasion for a family get-together. My grandma, Jayaba, age eighty-two, was visiting us. She met Reshma and really took a liking to her. That was a very special blessing.

The wedding date was fixed for April 15, 1995. The Hindu temple in Mauldin, South Carolina, was chosen for the wedding ceremony. The Shriners club in Greenville was selected for a reception in the evening. My wife Milan and Reshma went to India in February to shop. This was the same year I was chairman of the AAHOA. I was so busy I couldn't join them on the trip.

Shah family and friends had arrived at the Bermuda Run home to attend Mit's wedding. Saryu, my elder sister, her husband Chandrakant and their sons Sunil and Sandip, with their wives Rashmi and Mita and all the children arrived first. Malini, the baby sister, her husband Samir and sons Kaushal and Niraj were the next. My cousin Dhiren and wife Jayna arrived from Raleigh, North Carolina. Mohanbhai, Bhabhi and their daughter Ranju arrived from Daytona Beach, Florida. Their daughter Harshna came from Atlanta. Milan's sisters Jayshree and her husband Suresh and younger sister Damini and our close friends from all over the country arrived just in time to be present at the Musical Extravaganza pool party at the Bermuda Run home. After three days of partying, we were ready to head down to Spartanburg for the wedding ceremony.

The day before the wedding, both family groups arrived in Spartanburg where I was a partner in a Comfort Inn and a Day's Inn across the street. The Shah party occupied the Comfort Inn, the Patel party the Day's Inn. No outside guests were allowed for two days. At night we had an Indian folk dance, *garba*, at the temple. My nephews Sandip and Sunil, Sandip's wife, Mita, and their cousin Hemant were the performers on the stage. The two families, along with their relatives and friends, had one of the best *garba* nights ever at the Mauldin temple.

Bharat & Milan

On the morning of the wedding day, a white horse and a two-horse carriage were ready for the groom's procession. Mit was all decked in Maharaja attire. The Mauldin High School band was ready to play Indian music and walk in front of the procession. The frontage of the temple provided the best gathering spot for the groom's procession. All the ladies were decked in ornate saris behind the band, the groom was on a white horse, his female cousins were in the carriage behind him, the dancing guys and girls were in the center, and men were at the end—a typical Indian wedding scene! The neighborhood saw the procession and pulled out their cameras to film this once-in-a-lifetime event. The ceremony was performed in the temple. The priest pronounced Mit and Reshma husband and wife, and the two of them put garlands on each other. Tears rolled from my eyes, and I tried to wipe them carefully so no one would notice. After the final prayers at the temple, the newlyweds went to the hotel in a black limo. I thanked Mahendra for raising my new daughter, Reshma. He was moved immensely by my gesture.

Mit's Wedding

Everyone was given a map to the Shriners club in Greenville. Milan was in charge of the decorations. We left early to reach the club first. We followed the map. When we reached a T junction, I realized the map was wrong. We had to turn left and not right as the map showed. I called both the hotel desks and asked them to inform everyone as they left for the reception. We looked at the arrangements at the Shriners club and found everything in order. The guests were arriving slowly. Reshma, all decked up in her special reception dress, arrived with her family and friends. Now we were all waiting for Mit's appearance.

For about two and half hours, there was no news of Mit. He had left the hotel with his friend Scott. Milan and I started to worry and thought of the worst possible things that could have happened to Mit. There were no cell phones then and there was no way to contact him. I was angry with myself that I didn't bring him to the reception myself. I had promised myself, starting from Winston-Salem and to the end, that I would have Mit travel with me. I had kept that promise until that evening, and I hated myself for not following my own rule. Mit and Scott had followed the map and gone the wrong direction. They reached a Shriners club in another town and found it was the wrong place. They received the correct directions and finally made it to the waiting crowd. Immediately we went into reception proceedings, starting from the introduction of family members and then the newlyweds, Mitesh and Reshma Shah. My younger son, Raj, then asked everyone to enjoy the evening of drinking and dancing. Let the party begin!

My life had experienced many ups and downs, but never had I been shaken up like this for what had happened that evening. I felt relieved that Mit was safe, but somehow the thoughts of what could have happened to him did not leave me. I went to the bar and had three or four Scotches in succession. I walked out with another drink in my hand and leaned against a pole, gazing outward to the sky. I was truly shaken for the first time ever in my life. Milan felt my absence at the party and asked Mohanbhai to look for me. He found me on the front porch by myself and realized my pain. In a loud, commanding voice, he told me to shake it off and guided me inside.

The DJ, Lucky of New York, was doing a great job getting the whole crowd on their feet. The entire hall was a dance floor! Two bars, one on each end of the hall, were busy. When they started to close at midnight, Mohanbhai slipped hundred-dollar bills to the bartenders and asked them to leave it open until he said to close them. They not only left the bars open, but they joined the dancing party with the Indian music blasting the hall. The show went on until four in the morning. It was the best wedding party I have ever seen to date.

The Shah family was watching the movie of the wedding reception a month or so later. At one point, Mit asked me to rewind a little and play it again. As the scene rolled again, Mit and Reshma shouted together, "Dad, you were crying!" It was when they were putting garlands on each other and the cameraman scanned the crowd for a reaction shot. I was there, in the forefront, carefully wiping my tears that I now realized I couldn't hide. I told them it was the happiest moment of my life—and it really was!

My first greeting card to Reshma, written sometime during 1995, suggested I believed we had met before in our previous lives. Hindu philosophy suggests that family members remain together life after life in different relationships. Reshma must have been my own daughter in a previous life. Reshma and I have developed a very loving and caring relationship. My father had welcomed Milan into our family as Laxmi of his house, the goddess of wealth, prosperity, and happiness. Reshma is Laxmi of Bharat Shah's house. She has brought prosperity and happiness and is a pillar of peace within my family.

Right after the wedding, Reshma left for Cincinnati for her residency in family practice. Mit and Reshma's son, Arjun, was born in February of 1998. Reshma returned to Atlanta in June of 1998, with a baby boy. At that time she was preparing for her board exams. She would get up early, prepare a milk bottle for Arjun and feed him. Reshma would give Arjun to Milan for care taking and then leave for a library to study. After a couple of days of watching her schedule, I offered to take care of Arjun, warm up milk and feed him, so she could leave early to study. She loved the plan, and I enjoyed my morning grandfatherly chores. Arjun and I bonded to the point that he would anxiously wait for me to arrive. When I reached out to him, he would acknowledge my presence with a smile. For me this was the real joy of life! As Arjun grew, Milan and I would take him to a nearby park to run around and feed the ducks in a lake. Today, at age sixteen, he is a kind and mature young man, a serious basketball enthusiast who roots for Wake Forest, following his dad's footsteps.

Roshni, our granddaughter, was born in August of 2001. Reshma would drop her at a kindergarten, and I would pick her up. Roshni and I would sing songs when I was driving and she was in the back in a baby seat. I would teach her Hindi songs; she would teach me some from her kindergarten book. After teaching me how to sing a song, she would ask me to repeat it. I would purposely mess it up. She was a strict examiner; no mistakes were allowed! We would dream of going up into the sky. I would be Santa; she the reindeer. Again, a wonderful bonding and a simple pleasure of life. Today, at age twelve, Roshni is a mature young lady, very smart and focused.

The only desire Grandpa has is to live long enough to see Arjun and Roshni grow up, see them happy and immensely successful in their lives, and proudly announce that these are my grandchildren!

Grandchildren Arjun & Roshni

CHAPTER 25
Life's Biggest Lottery

On August 15, 2000, I was at the Emory Clinic for my general physical examination with Dr. Dipak Vashi, my good friend and personal physician. I got a call the very next evening from Dipak, asking me to come back for another blood test. The one that was done a day before didn't seem right. My white blood count was around 14,500; a normal count should be within the 5,000–7,000 range. The second blood test showed the white count at 27,000. Dipak suspected something amiss and arranged for me to meet Dr. Leonard Heffner, an oncologist, at Emory Hospital. A bone marrow sample was drawn by Dr. Heffner, and we waited a couple of weeks for the results.

The day we had an appointment with Dr. Heffner to get the results of the bone marrow testing, my sister Kunju and her husband, Vinesh, were visiting us from Surat, India. Milan and I left home, telling them we were leaving for Milan's eye examination and would return soon. Reshma, now a family practitioner, met us at Dr. Heffner's office. As the doctor explained the results of the test, tears began running down Reshma's face. I knew the news wasn't good. Milan saw it, too, and I could see that she was worried. I was diagnosed with having Chronic Myeloid Leukemia, CML. The choice of treatments was either chemotherapy or a bone marrow transplant. Regardless of the treatment, the doctor told me I had between six months to about three years to live. Time to "leave" was fast approaching. I, for some reason, was very calm. On our way home, Milan insisted that we tell Kunju of my diagnosis so she could give a sample of her bone marrow for a possible match. I insisted I didn't want any of my family members to know about this situation, and I prevailed.

The next day, when I reached the Noble office, Mit suggested we inform the staff about my health. I insisted that he hold off on making the announcement. I also told him that I had no fear of death; this was just a short part of a long journey. And by the grace of god, it's been a good one. I had thoroughly enjoyed my life. I had done the best I could do for my family and fellow human beings that I had come across. I had a loving family life with his mom, him, Reshma, Raj, and of course, my grandson, Arjun. Granddaughter Roshni was not born yet. I told him that Noble was in his capable hands and care. All I wished was for him to take care of his family, his mom, and his brother, Raj.

The Shah Family

The Internet and the access to information is the greatest thing in this day and age. Reshma's entire family—her father, her two sisters, and both brothers-in-law—are medical doctors. Each one of them, as well as my sons and I, jumped on the Internet and researched CML. What we found was that Novartis Pharmaceuticals of Switzerland was in the process of conducting clinical trials on a substance called STI-571 to see its effect on CML. A few newspaper articles had been published, remarking on the quick effect of STI-571. The *Good Morning America* show on ABC had conducted an interview with one of the patients and his doctor, Dr. Richard Silver of Weill Cornell Medical Center in New York. Brian Druker was a medical student in 1970s and had envisioned destroying cancer without devastating the patient through chemotherapy. Since 1970, many research scientists had developed theories on chromosome changes resulting in cancer. Dr. Druker had made contacts with the scientists at Ciba-Geigy during the late 1980s to formulate cancer treatments based on his and other scientists' results in the field. A few years had passed without much progress, while Dr. Druker continued honing his theory at Oregon Health Sciences University in Portland, Oregon. In 1993 Dr. Druker contacted the scientists at Ciba-Geigy, now a part of Novartis. He got them excited on new formulations based on molecularly targeted drugs. The scientists at Novartis sent several compounds to Dr. Druker to study. STI-571 was a clear winner in terms of its potency and selectivity. Phase 1 clinical trials began in June 1998, and the results were astounding. The Phase 2 study was initiated in 1999, and Phase 3 study began in the middle of 2000, with many laboratories in the United States and Europe participating with a larger and varied group of patients.

As members of my extended family researched CML, the decision was made to approach those clinics that participated in the STI-571 study. We found that Bowman Gray Medical Hospital, in my hometown of Winston-Salem, was one of them. The next closest one was Weill Cornell Medical Center in New York City, with Dr. Richard Silver as the chief investigator. To our surprise, Emory Hospital did not participate in the study. Within a few days, the family was in Winston-Salem for an appointment with an oncologist at Bowman Gray. I filled out the forms to enter the Novartis study. The forms were scanned and sent via computer to the Swiss headquarters. Within thirty minutes the results were back: I was put on the regular chemotherapy, Interferon treatment, not the STI leg of the study. This was a blind and random process where no one had control over the outcome. The doctor gave us the news, and we asked him to give us some time to make a decision.

Meanwhile, something else was going on. Reshma's sister Tejal was in New York at Long Island College Hospital for her residency in Radiology. Her fiancé, Anand, was also a resident in Radiology at Albert Einstein Hospital in New York. One afternoon, as Anand was discussing my case with the department head, Dr. Jacqueline Bello, a woman named Sara stopped by and listened to the conversation. Sara urgently needed a radiologist to read an image of one of her patients. She mentioned that she had overheard their conversation related to CML and that she knew a world-renowned expert in treating the disease, Dr. Richard Silver. Sara had worked for Dr. Silver for six years before joining the pediatrics department at Einstein. Anand explained the status of my sickness and requested if she could help to get an appointment with Dr. Silver. As Anand read the image for her patient, Sara got an appointment for me to see Dr. Silver. Before leaving for Winston-Salem, we knew that the following week I was to meet the man! While dwelling on the decision at Bowman Gray and not thoroughly appreciating the results of STI, I expressed my desire to take the chemotherapy treatment at Bowman Gray while staying at our own home at Bermuda Run in Winston-Salem. Raj put his foot down and insisted that considering how Anand had taken the trouble to arrange a meeting with Dr. Silver, we must go. We told the doctor at Bowman Gray that we really needed more time to think over the treatment and that we would be back in touch.

Bharat & Raj at Taj - 1998

On October 13, 2000, Milan and I were in New York at Dr. Silver's clinic. New blood tests and a bone marrow test were done. My white blood count had reached 55,000, ten times higher than normal. I was given medications to keep the white count under control and was asked to return the following week, when the bone marrow results would be available. Milan and I went back to New York on October 21, 2000. Before leaving Atlanta, I went to my prayer room. I was very calm while I recited my regular daily prayers. Then I remembered that a devotee had a right to demand a result from his spiritual guru, or even from God. I went to the photo of Rang Avdhut, my guru, and pointed a finger at him, demanding, "You better put me on the STI. You better!" All through my life, at every difficult moment,

I had only asked for blessings to overcome the present difficulty. I had never demanded that my wish be fulfilled. This was the first time ever I had Bapji in such a bind! I came down from the prayer room, and Milan and I got in a car and drove to the airport for our trip to New York.

At Dr. Silver's clinic, I filled out the forms to enter the study. The nurse, Maggie, filled out the blood and bone marrow test results and sent the request online to Novartis in Switzerland. Milan and I were sweating from nervousness in the lobby, and all of a sudden Maggie jumped up and shouted: "Oh my God, Mr. Shah, you better go and buy a million-dollar lottery ticket!" I asked her to calm down and to tell me what she had heard from Novartis. "You've been selected to go on the STI leg of the study!" she told me. I did not need to buy a New York lottery ticket; I had just won my life's biggest lottery. Dr. Silver came running to the lobby and hugged me. I was the third one to be on the STI leg among his sixteen patients in the study. He told me I would live longer than him! Milan and I walked to Weill Cornell Medical Center and met Judy Greensberg, research coordinator for Novartis. She gave us STI-571 capsules and asked me to start a 400 mg/day dose right away. We left for the airport with a three-month supply. We were in New York every ten days for blood testing. Each visit showed a reduction in white blood cells. By November 27, 2000, within two months of treatment, I was back to normal, with a white blood cell count of 5,300!

The effectiveness of STI on chronic myeloid leukemia patients at participating clinics was so startling that Novartis asked the US FDA and EU authorities to urgently consider its approval. On May 10, 2001, FDA approved the medication for the treatment of CML. The commercial name is Gleevec. All the test patients in the chemo leg were brought into the STI leg to save their lives. Gleevec is the only medication ever to be approved by the FDA within such a short time after a company's application for approval. Novartis has continued the study of STI-571 for the patients with CML, who had no other treatment before getting on the STI leg. I am one of them. Novartis wants to see a long-term effect of STI and to study resistance in the case of some patients who would have a relapse of the disease. Novartis has already developed an alternate therapy for those patients. Initially, I traveled to New York every month, then every quarter; and now, after being a part of the study for twelve years, the testing is done every six months. The test results have been excellent; the only side effects I experience are pale skin and bags under my eyes. Other than that, my life and my lifestyle have been normal and wonderful. An important fact remains that if I were not in USA and had I settled in India, I would not have received the STI-571 treatment. None of the hospitals in India participated in the clinical trials. The time to "leave" would have arrived a lot sooner! That is destiny. America My Destiny!

Bharat & Milan

Sometime in 2002, I had asked Tejal and Anand to contact Sara at the hospital and invite her for dinner during our next visit for the blood check. We met Sara and her husband at a restaurant. During the dinner, Sara told Tejal and Milan that she usually doesn't barge into someone else's conversation, and getting her patient's image read wasn't even that urgent. She said, "There had to be a purpose for me to be sent as a messenger, as an angel, to help Mr. Shah make a quick connection with Dr. Richard Silver." When I overheard Sara's comment, I knew my uncharacteristic demand of Bapji to get me on the STI treatment had been met!

In the summer of 2002, my brother-in-law Vinesh was sick with hepatitis. He and my sister Kunju lived in Surat, India. He was in and out of the hospital many times. Almost all the family members had gone to visit him, including my sister Saryu, who lives in Los Angeles, and my younger sister, Malini, who lives in New Jersey. Kunju was waiting for my visit in Surat and could not understand, as close as we were, why her big brother was not with her. After all, I had never told my siblings of my illness. The doctors finally gave up hope for Vinesh, and he was sent home. Kunju was filled with grief and cried all night long. I received a call from my niece, Dipti, for me to visit Surat and take care of my sister. I contacted Dipti's husband, Nirav, who was a pathologist in Surat, and explained my health situation. I told him that as much as I wanted to come, my family members in the United States were against the trip because I might get sick because of a compromised immune system. Nirav understood and concurred that I should not visit India, as diseases like malaria, typhoid, and bird flu were rampant and could be dangerous. Nirav visited Kunju and Vinesh and explained my health situation. I then called my sisters Saryu and Malini and explained my health situation. What I had feared did indeed happen: there was lots of concern and crying from my sisters. I am the only brother they have, as my younger brother, Sanjay, had passed away because of illness in 1972. Our parents passed away in the mid-1990s.

My brother-in-law Vinesh passed away within a year after he contracted hepatitis. Kunju visits us almost every three years. She travels first to New Jersey, where our younger sister, Malini lives, and spends some time with her. Then she goes to Los Angeles to stay with elder sister, Saryu. Finally, she arrives in Atlanta to see us. Within a week, both Malini and

Saryu arrive in Atlanta. We have family gatherings many times. As we all grew up in Navapur, my sisters and I have many funny stories about the townsfolk. So, just a mention of someone, and we all burst out laughing. And the stories go on nonstop! My family members call us "A Laughing Club." Deep down though, my sisters remain worried about their brother. Even though the STI treatment had been effective in controlling my leukemia, I was not sure of how long it would allow me to extend my life and lifestyle.

In September of 2012, Milan and I were in Dr. Vashi's office, going over the results of our general checkups. Everything looked good for both of us. Milan, with her family history of heart issues, asked Dr. Vashi if he would suggest coronary calcium score testing for her. He replied that it would be a good thing to do and wrote a prescription for her. Just as we were leaving his office, he looked at me and said that even though all my blood results were normal and that I had no family history of any heart-related issue, I should get the test done, too. If nothing else, it would be a part of my medical record. Where did this last second "supernatural message" come from? "She really does not need one; give it to him, he needs it". A week later, results showed that Milan was within the normal calcium range; however, I had hit the ceiling and required an urgent consultation with a cardiologist. Dr. Ashok Desai, a cardiologist and a good family friend, checked me and found all the tests to be normal, but he still did not like the level of calcium in my heart arteries. Dr. Desai contacted Dr. Nicholas Lembo, an angioplasty surgeon at Piedmont Hospital. Within two days, Dr. Lembo was putting stents on four major blockages, each one 90–95 percent blocked. While releasing me from the hospital, Dr. Lembo told me I was a "walking time bomb." In cardiologists' words, the condition is known as a "widow-maker." I could have dropped dead anytime, any day!

Bharat & Milan

This is the time to pause and to look at life going forward. Whatever is left of my life has to be enjoyed one day at a time. Milan and I have decided to tour every part of the world and keep a diary of our experiences, with plenty of photographs to fill the albums. The support of cancer research has been in the forefront of my efforts with financial contributions to the American Cancer Society. Dr. Richard Silver, who has played such an invisible but invaluable role in my life, is the founder and medical director of the Cancer Research and Treatment Fund in New York. I remain an active contributor to the institute's research efforts. I devote more time and money to charitable organizations dealing with the homeless, food for the hungry, veterans of wars, and assistance to seniors. I support educational activities at primary schools for the underprivileged in India. Giving back to my hometown, Navapur, I contributed toward an English medium school in honor of my mother, Indu, and a Teachers' Education College in honor of my father, Manubhai.

In the Hindu scripture, Geeta, Lord Krishna states that "the deeds done unselfishly, with a single-minded focus and absolute energy, will certainly bring desired goals. One should not be preoccupied with expected results before initiating an action. Get on with your work; leave the rest to the future, which is destined to be great anyway!" Milan and I understand the meaning of the teachings, and that is how we have always tried to conduct our lives. As individuals before marriage and then as a family, we have always tried to help anyone in need, without expecting anything in return. We have a routine of morning tea while sounds of prayers emanating from the home stereo system fill the surroundings. Sometimes, all of a sudden, this spiritual environment will bring up a topic for discussion. There is nothing, and I mean nothing, that we would complain of not having in our lives. Life has been a great blessing, and many miracles are a part of it. I believe the results of good deeds take time to come to fruition, but they always happen. Our good deeds have been paid back in abundance, multiplied many times over, and my daily prayers reflect my recognition and acceptance of those many blessings. It has been a very gratifying life indeed!

Bharat & Milan

CHAPTER 26
The Destiny

During early 1900s my grandparents Chunilal and Jiji had arrived in Navapur from a remote area of Gujarat looking for an opportunity for a better life for them and their children. Navapur was their destiny. Most of their children and grandchildren made Navapur their home. I came to the United States of America for a higher education. I saw a brighter future and took a chance of making my life better in this country. My sisters Saryu and Malini followed my path whereas our sister Kunju did not see the need to make a move and decided to stay in India where her family has done fabulously well.

During 1971, when I lost my first job at Nabisco Research Center, I had decided to return to India and once again try my luck there. A good friend advised me to stay for a while and look for another job. I joined RJR Foods soon thereafter. My younger brother Sanjay, at an young age of seventeen, was diagnosed with Hodgkin's disease and passed away in 1972. Except for chemotherapy, no other treatment was developed during those times. I was devastated when I arrived in Navapur to visit my family. Before I returned to the USA, I spent a few days in Bombay to discuss a job opportunity that would allow me to move back home to my family. This time, with a US degree and experience, it was easy to get an executive level job with a decent salary, car and housing provided by a company. My brother-in-law, Saryu's husband, Chandrakant, was with me. A day before leaving for the States, I received a handsome offer as a Chief Food Technologist with a company in Bombay. I told Chandrakant to let my father know that I would be moving to India in the near future. Being the only son in the family, I intended to take care of my parents. A telegram was waiting for me as I reached my apartment in New Jersey. International phone communication was very difficult during those days. My father's message was very clear: "Do not return to India. Letter follows". The letter arrived after a week where he detailed his reasoning. Daily hassle with corruption, unreliable corporate structure and a high level taxes on declared salary income were his main negative points. I decided to stay put.

The thought of returning to their home country is a constant process in the minds of new and old immigrants. What we miss is our family, friends, community and known surroundings. There is a period of adjustment in the new environment of culture and traditions. Those who participate within the local community to get to know the neighbors and colleagues, imbibe the new life, without sacrificing their own, get adjusted well. For others who just stick to their own lifestyles, assimilation in the new land is difficult. Also true is that it takes many trips back and forth to their own countries to realize that the grass looks greener only from far away. We start making notes of advantages and disadvantages of both the environments. There are many factors to consider while evaluating their effect on lifestyles. No one place would fulfill all the wishes. For us, the US immigrants, factors such as availability of daily amenities, scope of education for children, medical facilities and services, ease of travel, level of sanitation and a real sense of human rights helped us in making a final decision to put a stake in ground in the United States of America.

There are a few whose family businesses are well established and have good political connections in India. They have different goals. They come to the USA for higher education, work for corporate America to gain experience, and then return to India to help their family business grow. There are others, within the information technology field, who have seen opportunities in India and where government is eager to help, have established their businesses in India. Some have permanently moved there and have done well with their enterprises. Others have joined large corporations with international footprints and have been successful. As a matter of fact, a substantial number of Americans have found good base in India and have moved to India with their families. There are instances where the families have decided to move back to USA after 5-7 years of stay. In most cases the reasons are corruption at all levels, lack of infrastructure, sanitation, proper and timely medical treatments and children's education.

Recently, one would experience a sea change in all these aspects as the general population has awaken the policy makers and are demanding change as well as recognition of human rights and values. The country has moved far ahead in the world in its use of information technology for business and personal applications. Medical facilities and services have advanced to a point where India has been a preferred destination for medical tourism.

Many of us have entered the hospitality business in the USA and have made great progress. Our hearts would want to go to India and develop properties there. As the Indian economy has grown at a faster pace during last decade, there is a tremendous need for hotel rooms to serve the local and international business visitors. Many American hotel companies have undertaken management of new and existing hotel properties. Some AAHOA members have undertaken large and small hotel development projects, mainly in the state of Gujarat. The government of India has recognized the importance of non-resident Indians and encourages them to bring home investments in various fields. Programs such as Bhartiya Pravasi Divas are conducted specifically for the purpose.

Having seen the upcoming opportunities in India, sometimes we feel that being absent from our homeland we may have missed the mark to take advantage of the opportunities. The other side of the coin is also true that for those of us who have been in USA for a long time and are in tune with the life in this country have at last realized that the home is right here. Our children who are born and raised here rightfully feel that they are Americans and USA is their homeland. They have gone to school here and they follow basketball and football and not the game of cricket we remain attached to. Moving back to India at this juncture would make our children's life difficult as they would be strangers in their patents' home country. In keeping the balance between the cultures of both the worlds, we parents have made all the efforts to teach children their culture and religion, and have taken the task very seriously. During our visits to India, we have felt, to some extent, that our children's and grandchildren's understanding of our cultural and religious principles are much more superior to their Indian counterparts. Eventually what we have found is a balance between two lifestyles, India and USA. Many of us spend winter months in India where the weather is warm. It provides us an opportunity to maintain connectivity with family, friends and members of our community. We support worthy charities such as providing computers to local schools, nutritional meals to students, water works, hospitals and medical facilities especially in poor and rural areas. And when we return to the USA, we would miss India for a while but then the life goes back to the appropriate gear. We get busy with our work and businesses. There are growth opportunities in our own backyards with which we are more familiar and feel at ease in undertaking and completing projects. We have participated and are more attached to the projects in the communities where we have spent major parts of our lives. We get back to those projects. We support community based charities as we have a better feel of their needs. Usually our children are the movers of school activities and parental involvement is encouraged by the school officials. The family life moves ahead with those activities. We reconnect with the friends who were waiting for our return and life goes back to familiar fun and play. At the end, it certainly feels that we have returned home, a destiny that was meant to be!

CHAPTER 27
A Word to New Generations

Arjun & Roshni

Most of your grandparents who came to this country from India in the 1960s and 1970s came for higher education. All may have their life stories of fulfilling their American Dream not much different than mine. We all struggled for survival, with very little money in our hands. Regardless of our difficulties, we achieved our educational goals and worked in corporate America in professional fields. Later on, some of us who studied finance, information technology, and medical science ventured into our own enterprises. Some of us who entered the hospitality industry took an entirely different road than our educational background would indicate. We all started small, putting up every penny we had, not really knowing what our return on investment might be or even if we might get completely wiped out. But we were ready and willing to start all over again. Anyone can have that spirit, granted, but that spirit gets fostered more in this country, the United States of America, than anywhere else. As time passed, those of us who worked hard and smart and never wavered in our integrity reached heights leading to financial and personal freedom. These stories can only be told by us—and only in this good old United States of America! We prepared the ground, and your parents built solid foundations on it. Now we, as your grandparents, look at you to build solid structures on what has been handed over to you; and knowing your genes, we know you can do it.

When we left home to come to this country, we left our parents, grandparents, and younger siblings behind. Chances are we had been the breadwinners for the family. Until we got settled here and saved some money to send home for our family, they probably had a hard time making ends meet. Most of all, the emotional toll that our parents—especially our mothers—suffered is unimaginable, not knowing when their children would return home. These sacrifices have no match; one cannot put a value on them. Even after spending half a century away from home, we have not forgotten those sacrifices and hardships. We revere our parents and our grandparents. They taught us family values of caring for the elders and helping brothers and sisters in need. We have fulfilled their desires without expecting anything in return.

You have most likely not experienced how three generations of family live together. We have. The bonding that one gets with family members is totally a different experience. The American lifestyles of the early 1900s had all in their fabric as three generations of a family lived together. You have moved much further than that. Still, you will find a different degree of pleasure and peace of mind if you get to know us, your parents, and maintain relationships with your immediate and distant family members. If a need arises, give them a helping hand, take care of them. Life will feel a whole lot more worthwhile.

Education is the foundation for your growth and progress, and your family will do its utmost to give you the best education there is. One thing is for sure: no one can take away your education and knowledge. Wealth is like sand in a fist; one never knows how and when it slips away. So, regardless of your family wealth, pursue education to the highest degree. There again, follow your dream, but make sure at the end it brings money home. There is no need to waste time on things that can be developed as hobbies. If you have money, all those dreams can be fulfilled with passion and pleasure. Collect enough wealth to take care of the family, enjoy time together on vacations, contribute to charities, and help the community you live in. Most importantly, do not try to become filthy rich, either. It keeps you from enjoying life to the fullest. It places demands on your time that skew what is known as a balanced life. For sure, you will sacrifice your family life; your children will not get to know you, as you will not have time to love them. And that is no life at all.

Leadership in all endeavors is a trait you must develop. People around you need to know that they can count on you. Community involvement, Indian as well as American, will give you a sense of pride when you participate in a charity of your heart's desire and help someone in need. It will fulfill your life immensely. Get active in local politics to know and understand the issues facing the community, and seek practical solutions. Get to know and support the local politicians, as that network is of tremendous value in a time of need. Get involved in state or national politics only if you strongly desire it and have time to do it. Do not do it just to feed your ego as it is rough territory up there. The most rewarding activity is to get involved in your professional organization, the industry you represent. Reach to the top, even at a national level, to bring practical and ethical solutions to the issues facing the profession of your choice.

I have gone through six recessions in the last fifty years and have struggled through each of them. The one that started in 2008 was the harshest and most damaging. The cause of it can be summarized in one word: greed. I hope America has learned its lesson; I am sure it will. With all that has happened and whatever is lingering on, when it comes to the future of America, I am an ardent optimist. We shall overcome whatever difficulties lie ahead. Don't give up on America!

One last word: Once questioned on life's science and its interpretation by chemical, physical, and biological phenomenon, Albert Einstein suggested that there are many instances that can be explained, and there are a few that cannot; one can only surmise that they are divine intervention. I happen to fully agree with that summation.

During everyone's lifetime, there comes a point when life feels like a struggle, regardless of our education, our knowledge, and our hard, sincere work—it leads us nowhere. Frustration and depression set in; we feel lonely. The reason we feel lonely is because we have tried to fight it ourselves. If we have recognized a presence of divine power in our lives and its blessings on us, then the struggle and pain seem to ease away, because we are not fighting it alone. We may learn of a presence of a divine power at temples, churches, and mosques through spiritual discourses. The experience, the recognition, the acceptance only comes from within, at its own pace, in its own time. No one can force it upon you.

Daily prayers are a family tradition. An individual would pray in silence for a few minutes, each morning before starting daily activities and at night before going to bed. Which God an individual prays is a personal and a private matter. Important aspect is to make a connection with the Creator. A prayer gives one a peace of mind and provides focus for the task at hand. As one reaches spiritual depth, a realization sets in that one's existence is a miniscule particle in a vast universe. Human frailties such as jealousy, greed and ego come into control. Creating wealth for personal and family well being is of utmost importance in life. As one reaches that stage in life, one feels fortunate compared to other human beings who have financial, educational and health related weaknesses. Helping those humanities is our duty. That is karma. The philosophy of karma emphasizes the fact that good deeds never go unpaid; rather, the returns are manifold. That is the essence of life. Imbibe it, enjoy it!

We, your grandparents, wish you a lifetime of happiness!

Appendix

NAMES MENTIONED IN THE BOOK

Ahmedabad - City in the state of Gujarat
Amba - Hindu goddess prayed for strength, wealth and happiness
Ambaji - Town in Gujarat where Amba's temple is located
Amrutlal - Bharat's maternal grandfather
Amrut and Sumati Lala - Friends and partners in one hotel project
Anand - Our son Mitesh's brother-in-law
Arjun - Our grandson, Mitesh and Reshma's son, born February 1998
Ashok Desai - A cardiologist and a friend in Atlanta

Babu Patel - A friend in Greensboro, NC
Bapji - Guru Rang Avdhut's name, father, as the disciples addressed him
Baroda - A city in Gujarat where Milan went to college
Betty Kindred - Wife of Ted Kindred, Bharat's host family in Hyrum, Utah
Bhangrej - A doctor friend of grandfather Amrutlal
Bill and Linda Nabors - Bill was Bharat's classmate at Utah State University
Bill Wayman - Bharat's host and a banker in Logan, Utah
Bob Appleyard - Bharat's colleague at RJR Foods Inc., Winston Salem, NC
Bombay - Mumbai, a major city in India
Brahma - Hindu deity worshiped as a creator of world

Carol Conrad - Desk Clerk at Winkler Motor Inn, Winston Salem, NC
Chandrakant Shah - Bharat's sister Saryu's husband
Chandrakant Parikh - Bharat's friend in Bombay
Chunilal - Bharat's fraternal grandfather
Chuck Pheil - Director of Research at RJR Foods, Inc., Winston Salem, NC

Dilip - Bharat's friend in his hometown Navapur

Gujarat - A state in India

Gujarati - People from Gujarat and the local language spoken in the state of Gujarat
Gulab Shah - Bharat's friend from Wilson College, Bombay
Gulab Patel - Bharat's classmate at University of Tennessee, Knoxville, Tennessee

Indu - Bharat's mother

Jain - A person who follows the religion, Jainism
Jainism - A religion which is a different form of Hinduism. Followers of Jainism are strict believers of non-violence in all forms of life
Jiji - Bharat's grandmother, wife of Chunilal
Jim Myers - The owner of Winkler Motor Inn, Winston Salem, NC
J K Patel - Vice Chairman, Asian American Hotel Owners Association, 1995
Jayaba - Bharat's maternal grandmother
Jugal and Leena Shah - Bharat and Milan's friends in Rock Hill, SC

Kadod - Milan's hometown in Gujarat. Bharat's maternal grandparents also lived there
Kantibhai - Milan's father
Kantimama - Milan's father, addressed as maternal uncle by Bharat before marriage
Kindred - Ted and Betty Kindred, Bharat's host family in Hyrum, Utah
Kinu - Bharat's childhood friend
Krishna - Hindu god
Kunju - Bharat's sister

Lalit - Bharat's cousin and a friend from Bombay

Madhufoi - Milan's aunt in London
Mahendra and Ranjan Patel - Son Mitesh's in-laws, Reshma's parents
Mahesh - Hindu deity, also known as Shiva, a care taker of soul when a person dies
Mahesh Mehta - Bharat's friend and a roommate in Knoxville, Tennessee
Manju Bhoola - Milan's classmate and roommate at college in Baroda
Malini - Bharat's sister

Manu - Bharat's father

Manubhai - Bharat's father, "bhai" is added to the name to show respect

Mike Leven - Mike was very instrumental in the formation of Asian American Hotel Owners Association in 1986

Milan Shah - Bharat's wife

Milan Patel - Milan Shah's friend Manju Bhoola's daughter

Mit - Mitesh - Bharat and Milan's eldest son

Mohan Bhoola - Manju Bhoola's brother

Mohanbhai - Mohan Bhoola, "bhai" is added to the name to show respect

Mysore - City in south of India where Bharat went to study Food Technology

Najam Zainuddin - Bharat's friend and roommate at Logan, Utah

Nareshvar - Ashram of Bharat's guru, Rang Avdhut

Nathdwara - Town where Shrinathji (childhood form of Krishna) temple is located

Navapur - Bharat's hometown

Navin - Bharat's friend in Navapur

Olson - Bharat's research professor at Utah State University, Logan, Utah

Pardi - A town in Gujarat where Bharat's planned project to manufacture fruit juice powders was located

Pradip and Mira Shah - Friends in Parsippany, NJ

Punjab - A state in India

Punjabi - People of Punjab and the local language spoken in the state of Punjab

Raj - Rajesh - Bharat and Milan's younger son

Rajni - Rajnibhai - Bharat's cousin brother in Navapur, "bhai" is added for respect

Raman Madhav - RM - Bharat's friend at Wilson College, Bombay

Rang Avdhut - Bharat's guru

Ravji Chaudhary - Bharat's friend at Logan, Utah

Raxit Shah - Board of Director, Asian American Hotel Owners Association, 1995

Reshma - Son Mitesh's wife

Reshma Patel - Reshma's maiden name
Rita - Travel agent in Bombay
Richard Silver - Oncologist at Weil Cornell Medical Center, New York
Robert Joyce - Bharat's friend with political connections in North Carolina
Roshni - Our granddaughter, Mitesh and Reshma's daughter, born August 2001

Sagbara - A town in Gujarat where Bharat's father had invested for a lumber project
Salunkhe - Bharat's professor at Utah State University, Logan, Utah
Sanjay - Bharat's younger brother
Sara - A nurse at Albert Einstein Hospital, New York
Saryu - Bharat's elder sister
Satish - Bharat's friend in Navapur and a classmate at Wilson College, Bombay
Sadhna - A movie actress during 1960s in Bombay
Shankarbhai Patel - Bharat's friend in Nashville, Tennessee
Sharmila - A movie actress during 1960s in Bombay
Shrinathji - A childhood form of Hindu god Krishna
Sitaram Dakoria - Bharat's friend in Greensboro, North Carolina
Shiva - Hindu deity worshiped as a care taker of soul when a person dies
Surat - A city in the state of Gujarat
Suresh Joshi - Bharat's friend and a classmate at Wilson College, Bombay

Tarun Kapoor - Developed teaching courses on hotel management for Asian American Hotel Owners Association - 1995
Ted Kindred - Bharat's host family head in Hyrum, Utah
Tejal - Mit's wife Reshma's sister
Trinity - Philosophical manifestation of three Hindu gods, Brahma, Vishnu and Mahesh. Mahesh is also known as Shiva.

Ushaba - Milan's mother
Ushamami - Bharat addressed her as 'maternal aunt" before marriage to Milan

Vishnu - Hindu god as a preserver of life. Hindu gods Ram and Krishna are believed to be reincarnation of Vishnu

Vaishnav - A Hindu, follower of Vishnu

Wayman - Bill Wayman, a banker in Logan, Utah
Winkler Motor Inn - Winkler - Bharat and Milan's first hotel in Winston Salem, NC

Yash Paul Soi - Bharat's friend in Logan, Utah

Made in the USA
Columbia, SC
03 February 2018